AFRICAN BATTLELINE:
American Policy Choices
in Southern Africa

AFRICAN BATTLELINE:
American Policy Choices in Southern Africa

by WALDEMAR A. NIELSEN

Published for the
Council on Foreign Relations
by
Harper & Row, Publishers
New York and Evanston

The Council on Foreign Relations is a non-profit organization devoted to the study of political, economic, and strategic problems as related to American foreign policy. It takes no stand, expressed or implied, on American policy.

The authors of books published under the auspices of the Council are responsible for their statements of fact and expressions of opinion. The Council is responsible only for determining that they should be presented to the public.

For a list of Council publications see pages 153–155.

AFRICAN BATTLELINE:
AMERICAN POLICY CHOICES IN SOUTHERN AFRICA

Copyright © 1965 by Council on Foreign Relations, Inc.

All rights reserved, including the right to reproduce this book or any portion thereof in any form.

For information, address Council on Foreign Relations, 58 East 68th Street, New York 21

FIRST EDITION

Library of Congress catalog card number: 65-21376

Printed in the United States of America by Quinn & Boden Company, Inc., Rahway, N.J.

Published by Harper & Row, Publishers, Incorporated

M. K.
A. K.
In memoriam

IN MEMORY OF EDWARD JOHN NOBLE

The Policy Book series of the Council on Foreign Relations is published under a grant from the Edward John Noble Foundation in memory of Mr. Noble and his interest in encouraging American leadership.

Policy Books of the
Council on Foreign Relations

It is not always easy to discern where the crises of future years are brewing. But it takes no special gift of clairvoyance to foresee trouble in the southern part of Africa, where the confrontation of growing black nationalism and established white rule carries the threat of race war and international conflict. In some instances, notably in the Republic of South Africa, the whites are entrenched in power and show no sign of yielding or compromising. What the approaching crisis means for the United States, and what should be done in anticipation of it, are questions that deserve urgent attention today.

This is a subject full of complexities on which volumes could be written. The main forces at work, however, and the policy considerations which flow from them seem peculiarly suited to the format of the series of Policy Books of the Council on Foreign Relations. These books have a twofold purpose: first, to provide readers in this country and elsewhere with essays and analytical studies of the highest quality on problems of world significance; and second, to contribute to constructive thinking on American policies of the future. They are deliberately kept brief, not with the aim of simplification but to present with a minimum of factual background and detail the reasoned conclusions of individual authors with special experience and qualifications.

The Council was fortunate in persuading Waldemar A. Nielsen, President of the African-American Institute, to write this book. Mr. Nielsen came to the African field after many years of work in the affairs of Europe and the Far East. He knows Africa at first hand. He has served for the past two years as chairman of a discussion group on southern Africa which has met at the Council. Thus, he has had unique opportunities to observe and to assess the course of African developments.

In addition to the news and views which came out of the sessions of the discussion group, Mr. Nielsen had the benefit of the research assistance of Mrs. Annette E. Stiefbold and the advice and comment of a number of specialists invited to meet and discuss his manuscript with him. The Council wishes to thank the following, who were present at a special review meeting: Vernon McKay (Chairman), Ernest A. Gross, Thomas Hovet, Thomas Karis, Helen Kitchen, George Loft, John Marcum and Edwin S. Munger.

This is Mr. Nielsen's book. The views are his own, not those of the Council on Foreign Relations or of any group. The Council takes responsibility for the decision to publish it, believing it to be a significant contribution to thought on a subject of some urgency.

JOHN C. CAMPBELL
Editor

Contents

AFRICAN BATTLELINE:
American Policy Choices
in Southern Africa

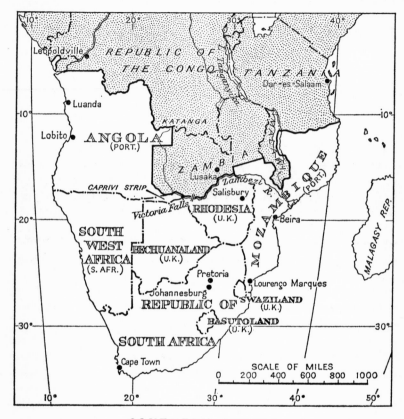

SOUTHERN AFRICA

Chapter I

Introduction

Across Africa today, a symbolic Battleline is traced. Beginning at its westernmost point, where the borders of the Congo and Angola meet on the Atlantic shore, it moves eastward and southward along Angola's frontier to Victoria Falls on the Zambezi. Thence it follows the great river downstream between Zambia and Rhodesia. At the border of Mozambique the fateful line leaves the river and snakes its way between that Portuguese province and Tanzania until it plunges finally into the Indian Ocean.

That twisting line is the moving edge of history. It is not a front where armies face each other in battle array. Rather, it marks the major political division of the Dark Continent today. To its north are the independent African nations, most of them born in a great tide of nationalism which since World War II has successively swept through North Africa, the arid Saharan reaches, the tropical rain forests, and the magnificent highlands of East Africa. To its south are eight countries or territories still controlled by white minorities but under siege by all the revolutionary ideas and influences of the contemporary world.

At the Battleline the wave of political transformation has stopped —perhaps only momentarily, perhaps for some time to come. But the struggle which it symbolizes proceeds continuously, on both sides of the line and even beyond the confines of Africa. Indeed, as many of its most important battles have been and will be fought in London, Lisbon, Washington, Moscow, Peking, and the halls of the United Nations as in Addis Ababa, Léopoldville or Johannesburg.

The African states to the north are increasingly insistent that colonialism and white domination of black populations be swept totally from their continent. Behind their insistence, even discounting for some opportunism and exaggeration in their clamor, the pulse and the heat of deeply felt resentments and convictions are unmistakable.

Southward of the line, likewise, the cords of tension are drawing more taut. Increasingly, the whites feel a sense of challenge if not of fear. In differing degree, black nationalist movements have begun to take form—organized and equipped for guerrilla warfare and sabotage in some areas, still divided and feeble in others.

The essence of the issue emerges starkly from the population statistics of the number of whites who control, and the number of non-whites who are controlled.[1]

	Whites	%	*Non-whites*
Angola	172,529	3.5	4,657,920
Mozambique	65,798	1.1	5,698,564
Rhodesia	177,124	4.6	3,631,356
Basutoland	1,926	0.3	638,748
Swaziland	5,919	2.5	231,112
Bechuanaland	248	0.06	320,427
South West Africa	73,464	13.9	452,540
South Africa	3,088,492	19.3	12,914,305

In their constitutional status there is great diversity among these areas. Some are in effect colonial dependencies of European governments; others have a considerable degree of self-government; and one, the Republic of South Africa, has been an independent state for many years, governed by its own white minority. In some— the so-called British High Commission Territories of Basutoland, Swaziland, and Bechuanaland—the principle of majority self-government is now accepted, and the remaining issue is largely a matter of the time schedule. In others, there is white resistance to black political advance, but it is poorly led and divided. In a cru-

[1] Source: United Nations Statistical Office and *United Nations Demographic Yearbook 1963* (New York: Author, 1964). The figures for Mozambique and Rhodesia have been revised according to more recent information. African population statistics are frequently unreliable, and widely varying estimates are published. Those given here should be interpreted as giving orders of magnitude.

cial few the controlling minority is disciplined, strong in its will to maintain its position, and powerfully equipped with the arms and apparatus to make its determination effective.

The region is uniform in only one characteristic: the present fact of white political control under challenge from black nationalism. There is no solid, integrated phalanx of white resistance; nor are the several African nationalist movements conducting their struggles in effective coordination with one another. There is consequently considerable complexity, but there is also a notable degree of flexibility and a range of possibilities for constructive action.

The impending struggles will shake all of Africa, and their repercussions may reach every part of the globe. The countries of this remote region, never before of substantial concern to the U.S. government, will soon confront American policy with a series of troublesome and dangerous problems which can be understood only in the context of the events which have taken place in recent years elsewhere in Africa.

Except for a few accessible areas on its periphery Africa generally was taken under colonial control by the European powers only eighty years ago. But the system then built did not last. Since 1945, and particularly since 1957, a large part of it has quietly, or in a few cases noisily, collapsed. By 1965 political control had passed to the black populations everywhere except in the southern tip of the continent, and almost one-third of the membership of the United Nations consisted of independent African states. The suddenness of these changes, however, was more apparent than real, for the forces undermining colonialism had been invisibly at work for decades.

Much of the impetus for change came from the European colonial powers themselves. From the beginning they seriously overestimated the economic importance of their African colonies. In the end these areas, with few exceptions, brought them only indifferent returns. Even in the nineteenth century British critics were beginning to call the colonies little more than "a vast system of outdoor relief for our upper classes." And in the twentieth century, with the advent of ideas of social and international responsibility for the welfare of the indigenous populations, the economic advantage of possessing colonies was still further reduced. Also, the fundamental drives which originally underlay European imperial expansion gradually lost much of their force. Many conservatives as well as liberals in the metropolitan countries lost their zeal for empire, and colonialism was increasingy regarded as an outworn survival of mercantilist-militarist outlook. The world, or at least the Western world, in the course of the first half of the twentieth century outgrew the mentality of colonialism and advanced beyond its political values.

The intellectual foundations of the European position in Africa had already begun to rot away when the consequences of World War II rammed the superstructure of colonialism and demolished it. As a result of the war Western Europe, gravely weakened economically and militarily, saw its dominant position in world affairs broken. Within Africa itself, the ferment of nationalism, which had been slowly growing for several decades, sharply accelerated. Hundreds of thousands of young Africans who had served as members of the allied forces were exposed to the ideas as well as the sacrifices of the war. Many returned home aggressively demanding new political rights.

Thus Europe in the postwar years found its position in Africa beleaguered on all sides—by African leaders and their growing nationalist following, by the Asians who strongly supported them, by the Soviet bloc, and, in a subtle and indirect way, by the general anticolonial attitude of the United States. Unwilling to pay the political and economic price of indefinite resistance to these multiple pressures and having joined the anticolonial ranks to a degree themselves, the European metropoles (with the notable exception of Portugal) gave way. Preparation for independence, or at least self-government, became the policy of several of the metropoles at that time.

The United Nations organization, created as the war closed, greatly facilitated the process of decolonialization. It served as the prism which brought the new ideological, moral, and emotional forces into focus. Though it played a relatively indirect part in effecting political changes, it provided the stimulus as well as the framework within which they occurred. These complex components produced a dramatic series of events which reached its climax in 1960 when no less than seventeen new African nations became

independent members of the United Nations. Immediately thereafter they began to play an active role on the world scene and to
affect the policies and calculations of the major world powers.

The American Relationship with Africa

Africa, in consequence of the slave trade, has profoundly marked
the nature of American society and the course of its internal development since colonial days. But as a serious concern of U.S.
foreign policy Africa is a continent which was not discovered until
some time after 1950.

Prior to the Second World War American concern with Africa
did not go much beyond criticizing the African policies of other
governments. It was the war itself that brought Africa into the field
of vision of American officials responsible for military and diplomatic affairs. The North African campaigns and the launching of
the invasion of Southern Europe from North African bases made
clear the strategic significance of at least that portion of the continent. The utility of African logistical and communications facilities,
the availability of African raw materials, and the presence of African support and combat units further impressed official American
thinking.

Coincident with the beginning of such awareness, however, came
a turn in the world situation which caused the United States to
subordinate its nascent strategic and political interest in Africa to
the immediate requirement of dealing with a menacing shift in
Soviet policy which had begun to manifest itself even in the clos-
ing months of the war. From 1945 onward, the United States and
its Atlantic allies were confronted with a rapid succession of Soviet
military and diplomatic thrusts in Europe, the Middle East and
Asia. By 1949 Communist forces had taken control of mainland
China; in 1950 the Korean War began; and in 1953, four years
after exploding its first atomic bomb, the Soviet Union acquired
thermonuclear weapons. In the face of such sustained, massive
challenge the United States as leader and financier of the Western
world had no choice but to devote itself, with utmost urgency, not
only to rebuilding its own military strength but also to helping
rebuild the economic and military capacity of its European allies,

sustaining their morale and promoting greater unity among them. During the critical years of the cold war and up to the late 1950s when the containment of Communist expansion was the dominant concern of the United States, the priorities of U.S. policy on a world-wide basis were clear—at least to the extent of putting Europe at the top and Africa near the bottom.

During this period the United States consistently followed the lead of its Western allies on African matters. Although it continued to express its anticolonial viewpoint from time to time, the tenor of American statements was carefully modulated to take into account European sensibilities. This line of American policy accorded sympathetic generalities to the Africans, but it heavily emphasized the virtues of "orderly transition from colonial to self-governing status" and on concrete issues it systematically deferred to the European metropoles. Indeed, almost until 1960 the United States acted on the premise that Africa was essentially a corollary and subsidiary aspect of its primary relationship to Europe.

During this period the cheerful belief was maintained in Washington that although political changes were brewing in Africa, the situation on the whole was quite satisfactory. In 1950 Assistant Secretary of State George McGhee wrote that ". . . it is gratifying to single out a region of ten million square miles in which no significant inroads have been made by communism and to be able to characterize the area as relatively stable and secure."[2] Within ten years, however, the political skyline of the continent had become almost unrecognizable. To many critics it seemed clear that American awareness of the political realities of Africa had been dangerously obscured by preoccupations in other parts of the world, and that U.S. policies had been overtaken by "the wind of change."

There was undoubtedly some truth in such an interpretation; and seen through African eyes, American policy toward Africa in the crucial years from 1946 through 1960 was grievously negligent and defective. Viewed from a world-wide perspective, however, it achieved its primary objective, namely the protection of essential U.S. and Western security interests. Granted that it was largely a policy of equivocation, neutrality, and passivity. Granted also that

[2] *Department of State Bulletin,* June 19, 1950.

it was entirely satisfactory to no one, neither African nor European. By attempting to remain in rapport with both disputants on many issues the United States became inevitably a target of criticism for both. To Europeans, the United States presented a mild but constant and irritating influence pushing them toward concessions to African demands for self-determination. To Africans, U.S. policy seemed flabby and disappointing at the critical moments in their struggle for national independence. From an American viewpoint, however, the crucial test of the policy followed must be whether the losses in prestige or the irritation caused our allies were so great as to produce palpable and enduring damage to U.S. interests. By this measure it was successful. It did not lead to serious ruptures in the Western alliance during the period of greatest threat from Soviet expansionism. And when the alliance eventually began to weaken, the causes were related primarily to factors other than differences over Africa. With respect to African relations, almost without exception the United States has been able to work effectively with the new governments subsequent to their independence even though it did not play a vigorous role in support of their liberation.

The United States and Independent Africa

During the most active period of the independence struggles in northern and tropical Africa, the United States was largely immobilized by its contradictory interests and responsibilities in Europe. But once independence in any country was won, it moved reasonably quickly into action.[3] Spurred in part by the promptness of Soviet diplomatic recognition and offers of aid, the United States has made haste in recent years to relate itself directly to the new states and to give them substantial assistance for economic, educational and social development.

This policy in turn has necessitated changes in the organization and staffing of U.S. government agencies both in Washington and in the field. In mid-1958 the Department of State for the first time

[3] In Sierra Leone, Nigeria, Ghana, the Congo (Léopoldville), Togo, and Madagascar, the United States commendably set up official representation even before independence.

created a separate bureau of African affairs. At that time fewer American diplomatic and consular officers were stationed in the whole of Africa than in the German Federal Republic alone. But by 1965 thirty-four embassies and twenty-one consular establishments were operative in thirty-nine African countries. In the same brief period other branches of the government have also moved to reorganize and expand their African staffs and programs. In step with growing official interest, American foundations, universities, and private organizations of many kinds have initiated programs of educational and technical assistance. The American press and television have begun to give increased coverage to African developments, and sections of the American public have become caught up in the excitement of Africa's political emergence. The period of American indifference to and ignorance of Africa has come at least to the beginning of its end.

Parallel with new interest and new programs in Africa came a change not so much in the content as in the tone of U.S. policy. By 1959 the United States had begun to mute its reiteration of the dangers of "premature" independence and to stress the positive potentialities of the newly independent states. By 1960 official spokesmen had largely turned from cautioning African nationalist leaders against impetuousness to "welcoming any steps" taken by the European metropoles to prepare their African dependencies for self-government. Similarly, American preoccupation with the Communist threat in Africa had begun to lessen, as well as American disapproval of "neutralism" on the part of African states.

The election of President Kennedy in 1960 accelerated this evolution of U.S. policy. As a senator, Mr. Kennedy had served as chairman of the African Sub-Committee of the Foreign Relations Committee, and he had on several occasions declared his antipathy to colonialism. As President he encouraged officials of his administration to speak out on African issues more boldly than ever before. This was a period of rising sympathy in the United States for African needs and of American optimism about the continent's future and prospects. But the eruption of crisis in the Congo in 1960, and the continuing problems of that vast and rich but invertebrate country have subsequently aroused new hesitancy and ambiguity in American policy.

Immediately after it had been precipitated into independence by a sudden reversal of Belgian policy, the Congo was confronted with a triple calamity: a breakdown of civil order, powerful attempts of foreign intervention, and the armed secession of Katanga and other provinces. The United States gave full political, logistical, and economic support to a U.N. effort to help the fledgling government in Léopoldville deal with these problems. This line of policy, though it proved reasonably successful, aroused deep misgivings and dispute in the United States and produced new strains in the Atlantic alliance.

American power and prestige had been committed for the first time in tropical Africa—and a number of influential persons within and outside the government were disquieted, if not horrified, by the implications. They felt the United States stood in danger of being drawn into an endless, costly and ultimately futile set of African commitments, possibly far beyond its interest and responsibilities, and distracting to its obligations in other parts of the world, including the war in Viet-Nam. U.S. and U.N. involvement in the Congo was subsequently reduced, and the government of Cyrille Adoula promptly collapsed. In an ironic turn of events, Moise Tshombe, the former leader of the Katangan secession movement, became prime minister in July 1964, thereby stirring new currents of concern and discord on all sides. Armed rebellion broke out in the northern and eastern areas of the country, and in late 1964 the Congo situation came to its second crisis as far as American policy was concerned.

In November of that year the United States joined with Belgium in an airborne operation to rescue several hundred whites then held as hostages by rebel forces in the vicinity of Stanleyville. The paratroop landing, generally seen as a humanitarian effort in Western Europe and the United States, provoked a spasm of outrage in much of Africa and led to a series of reckless and even racist attacks on the United States at the United Nations and elsewhere. The effects on American opinion, and the implications for American policy toward Africa, were far greater than was commonly appreciated. For Stanleyville and its aftermath were not seen or interpreted as an isolated event. Occurring in the wake of a general movement toward one-party states in independent Africa, spreading signs of internal instability and breakdown, and increasing evidence of Chinese and Soviet intrusion throughout the continent, it aroused serious misgivings about the pace of political change in Africa and the future prospects of stability. It has led to profound re-examination of some of the basic assumptions of American policy.

The new administration of President Johnson took office at this moment of anxiety and reconsideration regarding independent Africa. In this same atmosphere, the problems of southern Africa now begin to loom over the horizon of international concern.

Southern Africa: The Coming Test

The impending problems of southern Africa are in a sense the direct outgrowth of political developments which have taken place to the north and will be deeply affected by the new and disturbing course of events in that region. But in one extremely important aspect they are likely to be a new departure. The process of decolonialization in Africa has so far been remarkably bloodless. Algeria was a major and tragic exception; but on the whole, African independence has been agitated, argued, and negotiated for. It has not had to be battled for. In southern Africa this is not likely to be uniformly the case. In some areas, notably Basutoland, Swaziland, and Bechuanaland, an open dialogue exists between the Africans and the colonial government, and evolutionary movement can be anticipated. In Rhodesia the polarization of the situation is far advanced, but a solution other than open fighting may still be found. Here, as in the High Commission Territories, there is present a moderating factor in the form of a metropole committed to a nonviolent transition to self-rule based on equal rights for all inhabitants and universal suffrage. Similarly in South West Africa, because of its special international status, some constructive solution may emerge. But in three large, populous and important areas, Angola, Mozambique, and South Africa, the possibility of peaceful change is debatable. The internal situations, already hard, are hardening further. Frustration is growing, both on the part of nationalist elements within and on the part of the independent African states without. Thinking on all sides—white officials, African nationalist leaders, and interested outsiders—moves toward the anticipation of, and preparation for, tests of force.

When and if the flash point is reached will of course vary from country to country and be influenced by many factors—the speed of the intensification of repression and resistance, the outcome of issues before the United Nations, the readiness and capacity of the independent African states to force a showdown, the skill and courage of the several nationalist movements and their leaders, and the availability of material and other support from non-African sources. But if violence occurs, because modern weapons and millions of persons may be involved, it will not be on a minor scale.

Politically, the crucial fact about such an eventuality is that the struggle would be between blacks and whites, and in a context in which the blacks would be fighting in behalf of moral and political principles which have stirred and shaken human events throughout the twentieth century—self-determination, democracy, human rights, and racial equality. Thus, by the nature of the case, the struggles would engage the emotions of a large majority of the world's population. Moreover, because of the powerful psychological and symbolic factors involved, they would offer important and irresistible attraction to both hemispheres of the Communist world, the Russian and the Chinese.

For the United States the challenge is therefore likely to be severe. In the still-flexible situations, as the High Commission Territories, the posture which has hitherto been adopted in the regions to the north may continue to be serviceable; but in the crucial, impacted situations of the south, fundamentally new approaches will be required. Hitherto it has been possible for the United States to attempt to reconcile its intersecting European and African interests by avoiding or deferring clear choices. But in Angola, Mozambique, and South Africa, middle ground is disappearing, and the stark outline of ultimate alternatives becomes progressively more visible through the murky atmosphere of dispute. Moreover, through the Organization of African Unity (OAU) and the United Nations the independent African states appear determined to force the United States to make sharper choices in southern Africa— between Portugal and the independent African states, for example, or between the protection of its economic interests in southern Africa and the preservation of its assets and future economic opportunities in the independent areas to the north.

The stalemated situations of southern Africa are not yet in their final form; but they are approaching their climax. Consequently, the time when a policy of equivocation, detachment, and passivity could adequately serve American interests is rapidly passing.

Southern Africa is only one of several troubled regions of the world which may confront the United States with hard policy choices having wide ramifications. But because of the acuteness of the moral issues in the struggles which may erupt, and because of their deep emotional implications for much of mankind, they present especially great dangers to peace and stability, and thereby to American interests. Chief among these may be their effect in accelerating an emerging North-South division of the world on the basis of wealth and of race and in injecting the ominous factor of color irrevocably into world politics.

Already the division becomes visible as the gap between the rich and the poor nations widens, as the wealth of the developed areas vigorously expands while economic progress in the less-developed areas lags. Moreover, color increasingly correlates with poverty, forming a culture of distress and resentment in which racism can quickly breed. A brutal and protracted struggle of blacks against whites in southern Africa could in the future make race the divisive factor in international affairs which ideology and religion at other times have been.

Racial conflict in southern Africa could bring other deplorable consequences. It could envenom relations between all the Western nations and the underdeveloped world. It could endanger the stability of all of Africa. It could turn black nationalism decisively toward the Communist powers, more particularly toward China. It could gravely affect the role, even the existence, of the United Nations. It could seriously complicate the relations of the United States with certain of its European partners. In particular, if American policy and diplomacy prove inadequate to the challenge, the results could deeply corrode the influence and world leadership of the United States. For the issues involved touch directly the basic principles and values upon which the American political system and society have been built and upon which its moral and spiritual prestige rests. The fact that the United States itself is in the midst of historic efforts to deal with its internal race problem at the moment when southern Africa threatens to explode only accentuates the American dilemma. Like slavery in the nineteenth century and Nazism in the early twentieth, the issue of human and political rights for the black majorities of Africa poses ultimate choices for nations as well as individuals, choices whose consequences for good or ill will ripple outward to the ends of the world and resound for generations.

This short book attempts to review the issues and policy choices confronting the United States in each of the several parts of southern Africa, beginning with Angola, Mozambique and Rhodesia, which form the southern side of the Battleline, then proceeding directly to the central case of South Africa, followed by discussion of the problems of the High Commission Territories and South West Africa which are directly related to it. In the concluding chapter, the interaction of the separate problems of the region and various overall considerations of American policy will be analyzed. Throughout, the steady objective is to derive specific and feasible suggestions for American policy. The temptation will be resisted, in dealing with these many emotionally charged issues, merely to strike dramatic and moralistic postures, or to forget that foreign policy as a branch of politics is also the art of the possible.

Chapter II

Angola and Mozambique

Two areas controlled by Portugal, Mozambique on the eastern side and Angola on the western, form the present anchors of the Battleline. According to the recent pattern of change in Africa, they should now be beginning to give way to the advance of independence. Their contiguity to the almost solid phalanx of black-controlled states to the north, their relatively small number of permanent white settlers, and the poverty and weakness of their metropole, Portugal, would all seem to point toward the relatively prompt transfer from dependent to independent status.

But in fact the change may not be imminent; and if the movement of independence is stopped for an extended period at the gateway they form, then the pace of all political developments to the south will be deeply affected. With a reprieve of a few years, new patterns of collaboration and collective defense could emerge among the remaining white-controlled areas, and even new forms of counterattack. In turn, new currents of frustration in the Angolan and Mozambican nationalist movements and among the countries to the north could produce steadily greater danger of violence and the greater involvement of non-African powers in the struggle.

For American policy Angola and Mozambique present some of the same complex problems and alternatives which are characteristic elsewhere in southern Africa, plus one major and special dilemma. Portugal is a member of the North Atlantic Treaty Organization. In a particularly acute manner, the struggle in Angola and Mozambique poses choices for the United States between a present ally and potential future friends, between security interests in a direct military sense and national interest in a broader political sense.

The Setting and the Reality

Though similar in their political links to Portugal, the two areas are markedly different in geographical and economic respects. Angola, with an area of 481,000 square miles, is the fifth largest country on the African continent. It is sparsely populated with some 4.8 million inhabitants, of whom 173,000 are Europeans. Of all the Portuguese overseas territories, Angola is the most important economically. The land is productive, with upland areas well suited to European settlement. The principal products are iron ore, diamonds, petroleum, fish and coffee. The last, accounting for 35 per cent of current exports, is an important earner of foreign exchange for Lisbon. To date the territory's mineral, hydroelectric and agricultural resources have been only partially developed, and research findings suggest that the long-term economic potential is formidable.

Mozambique is smaller in area but somewhat more populous. Of its 5.8 million inhabitants, some 66,000 are European. Economically it is less important to Portugal than Angola. Primarily an agricultural country without notable mineral resources, Mozambique's principal exports are cotton, sugar, copra, cashew nuts, tea and sisal. In addition, it receives important income from two "invisible" exports, namely, revenue from the transit traffic to and from the interior of the continent through its ports and over its railroads, and from the remittances of the 200,000 or more Mozambican workers employed in South Africa.

In strategic terms, the importance of Angola and Mozambique for all of southern Africa is very great. Each constitutes a land barrier, or link, between independent and white-controlled Africa. Lobito, the chief port of Angola, is of key importance because it is the terminus of the Benguela Railway, a system that serves not only the highlands of central Angola but also the Katanga region of the Congo. The railroad carries a large percentage of the heavy cargo of the Congo's portion of the African Copperbelt, and potentially it could carry a sizable part of the traffic from Zambia as well. Mozambique's excellent port, Lourenço Marques, is a major outlet for the agricultural and mineral products of South Africa, Swaziland, and Rhodesia. Beira, the second most important port, is connected by rail with the landlocked areas of Malawi, Zambia, and Rhodesia, and is a major facility for the traffic of the Zambian portion of the Copperbelt.

Thus, Angola and Mozambique have a powerful grip upon the economic life of the countries of the interior. Until and unless some of these countries are able to develop alternative transport routes for the bulk of their products and imports—which will be costly and difficult at best—Portuguese control of presently indispensable ports and railroads will have a clearly evident effect, not only on the economic life but also on the political behavior of all the peripheral states, both independent and white-controlled.

Portugal has been a colonial power on the continent ever since Portuguese navigators first visited Angola in 1482 and Mozambique in 1498. From then until the early nineteenth century trading in slaves was the primary Portuguese interest, those taken from Angola being supplied to the Americas and those from Mozambique being sent to the East. Portuguese settlement and trade were long concentrated on the coastal areas and little attempt was made until recent decades to penetrate and pacify the up-country regions.

Over the centuries, Portugal's hopes for and benefits from its African territories have waxed and waned. But since the advent of Dr. Antonio de Oliveira Salazar to power in the 1930s, and more particularly since World War II, Portugal has taken a determined interest in them and has formulated an elaborate rationale or mystique for its relationship to the areas and to the native populations. In its motives in becoming a colonial power in Africa and in the harshness of the administration of its territories, Portugal has been little different from, and perhaps no worse than, some other European countries. But Portugal, which has not accommodated itself to African nationalism as have the others, envisages its purposes, role and accomplishments in highly distinctive terms.

First, the asserted goal of colonial policy has long been to integrate the native peoples into the Portuguese nation. In sharp contrast to the philosophy of apartheid, for example, the Portuguese have held out to the African the possibility of gaining the same rights and privileges as a born Portuguese, once he acquired what the Portuguese have defined as a "civilized" way of life. The territories in Africa, therefore, are not regarded as colonies. They are by constitutional law "provinces," parts of Portugal.

The Portuguese point with great pride to what they consider to be their acceptance of indigenous culture and their willingness to allow those Africans who so desire to become assimilated to Portuguese culture. This tolerant attitude, so the Portuguese believe, is the logical result of historical and social patterns which have long set their country apart from other colonial powers. According to Dr. Salazar, "because it was in a multi-racial type of society that we constituted ourselves as a nation eight centuries ago . . . we have been left with a natural inclination . . . for contact with other peoples. These contacts have never involved the slightest idea of superiority or racial discrimination." [1] He has frequently reiterated that a multiracial society is envisaged in the territories and that "no contribution of any one group should be excluded in the name of racism. . . ." [2]

A second and related characteristic has been an acute sense of mission in civilizing and Christianizing the African. Portugal sees itself, often in grandiloquent terms, as carrying what was formerly known as the white man's burden. "As a nation," says Dr. Salazar, "we are the trustees of a sacred heritage; we consider that it is our duty, and to the interest of the West, to safeguard it, and we sacrifice ourselves by fulfilling that duty . . ." [3]

This sense of duty, the Portuguese insist, has always outweighed economic considerations in their administration of the African territories. They cite the Native Statute of 1954, which describes the goal of Portuguese policy as follows: "The State shall endeavor by every means to improve, both materially and morally, the living conditions of the indigenous inhabitants . . . and . . . to educate them . . . by transforming their primitive usages and customs, directing their activities into useful channels, and actively integrating

[1] Interview with Premier Salazar, *Life* Magazine, May 4, 1962.
[2] Interview with Premier Salazar, *US News and World Report*, July 9, 1962, p. 79.
[3] Speech by Premier Salazar, quoted in *The New York Times*, August 13, 1963.

them into the community. . . ." [4] In this authoritative statement, which obviously reflects some concessions to the anticolonial trend of world opinion, certain uniquely Portuguese ideas are preserved behind the carefully chosen phraseology. There is a strong and consistent belief, plainly visible in the actual administration of Angola and Mozambique, that it is essential to inculcate Africans, forcefully if necessary, with an appreciation of the virtues of discipline and hard work. As a former colonial minister, Vieira Machado, has said, "It is necessary to inspire in the black the idea of work and of abandoning his laziness and his depravity if we want to exercise a colonizing action to protect him. . . . If we want to civilize the native we must make him adopt as an elementary moral precept the notion that he has no right to live without working." [5]

In every society there is a gap or lag between stated goals and economic and social realities. Between the verbiage of Portuguese policy and purposes in Africa and the actual condition of the native populations there is not a gap but a gulf.

It is true that the multiracial aspect of Portuguese policy and culture in the African territories has created relatively favorable conditions for racial integration. In contrast to the formerly French and British areas, both Angola and Mozambique have a relative lack of an official color bar, and miscegenation has created a small but significant mulatto population now estimated at more than 60,000.

But in other respects, Portuguese policy of cultural assimilation has been an overwhelming failure. Despite the legal possibility of achieving *assimilado* or full citizenship status, the number of Africans who were able to meet the requirements prior to the reform of the system in 1961 was pathetically small: less than one-half of 1 per cent of the total African population. In education, Lisbon's policy has not brought Portuguese culture or even literacy to the vast number of non-whites. Portugal has largely left the task of education and the "moral improvement" of the Africans to religious bodies, primarily the established Roman Catholic Church, with results which reflect little credit upon Portugal or the Church.

[4] Quoted in U.N. Document A/5160, August 15, 1963, para. 100.
[5] Quoted in James Duffy, *Portuguese Africa* (Cambridge: Harvard University Press, 1959), p. 318.

A double standard in educational facilities has been maintained, with nothing more than the most rudimentary educational opportunity available to African children. As late as 1962 the rate of illiteracy in Angola and Mozambique stood at 95 and 98 per cent, respectively.

If the Portuguese have done little to infuse the African with Portuguese culture, they have made a most determined effort to force him to work and to exploit his labor for the benefit of the state and of private economic interests. Before the advent of Dr. Salazar to power, Portuguese practices of slavery and forced labor in its African colonies produced repeated international outcry from humanitarian groups. Dr. Salazar's "New State" passed legislation in the 1930s which softened somewhat the barbarity of earlier practices and provided theoretical protection to the African against the exploitation of his labor. But even these laws, which prevailed until very recent years, were something less than models of enlightened social practice. Under them the African could be obliged by territorial authorities to work on public projects without compensation. In addition, he was subject to recruitment by the agents of private companies for contract labor, either within the territories or abroad, if he were found to be "indigent."

Compulsory and contract labor has provided hundreds of thousands of workers at extremely low cost for the mines, farms, and factories of Angola and Mozambique, as well as tens of thousands more for the farms and mines of South Africa. In the recruitment of workers, collusion between officials, local chiefs, and private companies was common, and the mistreatment of workers was widespread. The harshness of the system is suggested by the fact that to escape its requirements, more than a million Angolans and Mozambicans fled to work and reside in adjacent countries.

The contract labor system has been strongly criticized even by some Portuguese officials. Captain Henrique Galvão, well-known recently as a political opponent of Dr. Salazar, was in earlier years an Inspector General of Overseas Territories for the government. In that capacity he wrote in the late 1940s:

> From a realistic point of view, the situation is at least as inhuman as it was in the days of pure slavery. Yet in those days the Negro,

bought as a work animal, constituted a piece of personal property which his owner had an interest in keeping healthy and strong, just as in the case of his ox or his horse. Now the Negro is not bought but is simply rented from the Government without losing the label of free man. The employer cares little whether the man lives or dies, provided he keeps on working while he can; for the employer can demand that another laborer be furnished if the first one becomes incapacitated or dies.[6]

Until the institution of reforms in 1961, conditions in the Portuguese territories from the viewpoint of the African inhabitant were as bad as could be found anywhere in Africa. Although the racial doctrines of Portugal were more palatable than those of South Africa, he was still a victim of white domination and colonial exploitation in the worst sense of those terms.

Thus, assuming the sincerity of the Portuguese intent to "endeavor by every means to improve both materially and morally, the living conditions" of the Africans and to transform "their primitive usages and customs," a more total failure of a colonial effort can hardly be imagined. Portugal's ideal of native populations practicing Christianity, speaking Portuguese, deeply imbued with Portuguese culture, and bound to the mother country with strong feelings of love and sympathy, has become a dangerous self-deception. Except for some Portuguese, therefore, no one has been surprised to see, despite the backwardness of the territories, recent stirrings of nationalism and revolt.

Nationalism, Rebellion, and the Portuguese Response

On February 4, 1961, the Portuguese dream in Africa fell apart. Until then, despite minor manifestations of native discontent and the formation of various small nationalist political groups, Portugal had been able to maintain the illusion that the Africans in its colonies were contented and more desirous of being Portuguese than independent. It had been able to resist Afro-Asian efforts to bring about a change in its colonial policies and had managed to

[6] "Report on Native Problems in the Portuguese Colonies," reprinted in Henrique Galvão, *Santa Maria: My Crusade for Portugal* (Cleveland: World, 1961), p. 64.

persuade both Britain and the United States to vote against a series of U.N. resolutions directed against its administration of the territories. Within Angola and Mozambique, by a steady increase in the repressiveness of police measures, disturbances had been kept under control and the façade of stability held in place.

But on that night of February 4th, several hundred Africans in Luanda, the Angolan capital, stormed the police barracks. In the ensuing rioting, twenty-four Africans were killed, a hundred were wounded, and another hundred arrested. No sooner had the disorders in Luanda been suppressed than northern Angola exploded in scenes of terror and counterterror. In the months that followed, several hundred whites and many thousands of blacks were killed. The counterterror was carried out in part by the bombing of villages and the burning of broad areas by Portuguese military forces, but in large part it was the work of white vigilantes who had been issued arms by the government and whose excesses finally distressed even the territorial authorities.

By the time the smoke had cleared, nothing was the same. Conditions in the colonies had been openly exposed to world view, despite the most active Portuguese efforts to rebuild a propaganda screen around them. The United States and Britain had drawn back from support of Portugal at the United Nations. The nationalist movements of both Angola and Mozambique, previously small and splintered, grew rapidly and consolidated. And by the summer of 1961 the Portuguese Overseas Ministry was already instituting changes in administrative policies. Minimum wage standards were set, labor inspection procedures were adopted, minimum working ages for minors were established, and the practice of forced labor was abandoned. But since contract labor is not forced labor under Portuguese terminology, and since some of the most severe and criticized practices have occurred with respect to the former, these new measures represented a marginal improvement at best.

Another much publicized change was the elimination of the so-called *indigenato* status for all those Africans who juridically had not reached "civilized" or *assimilado* status. Legally the change meant that all Africans would henceforth be considered Portuguese citizens and would be dealt with under ordinary civil law. The principal practical effect was to increase slightly the number of

Africans able to vote. Beyond that, the meaning of the gesture is debatable.

Regardless of the immediate and specific effect of these changes, they were of great significance in the larger political context. To Africans and to the world, they meant that Portugal had begun to yield under increasing pressure of criticism; and that although it had been totally unresponsive to persuasion or negotiation, it had reacted quickly to a physical threat to its control in the colonies. In brief, force and violence were apparently the key to the political future of the areas. Recognition of this bald and unpleasant fact led to rapid developments both on the nationalist and on the Portuguese side.

In the following months, several Angolan nationalist groups joined under the leadership of Holden Roberto to form an Angolan Revolutionary Government in Exile (GRAE), which worked actively to develop a mass base of political support. Its military arm, the Angolan Army of National Liberation (ALNA), acquired arms and training facilities and by late 1963 had some 7,500 guerrilla troops in the field.

Consolidation and organization of the Mozambican liberation movement likewise followed, though somewhat more slowly. In early 1963, Dr. Eduardo Mondlane left a university teaching post in the United States to set up political headquarters in Dar-es-Salaam, Tanganyika. He succeeded in uniting the major nationalist groups into a new Mozambican Liberation Front (FRELIMO) and laid the basis for a Mozambican Liberation Army. He has vigorously presented the Mozambican case before the United Nations and enjoys the support of the Organization of African Unity. A distinctive feature of his policy has been heavy emphasis on the training of a cadre of qualified younger persons to carry the non-military responsibilities of the movement. By late 1964, the first reports of guerrilla fighting in Mozambique began to appear in the international press.

Since 1961, Portugal has thrown its fullest energies and resources into re-enforcing security forces in the two areas. The secret police has been strengthened, and efforts to detect and destroy all African political activity have become increasingly effective. New airfields have been built; border zones, particularly in northern Mozambique, have been burned and cleared; and in consequence, more than two hundred thousand Angolan and Mozambican refugees are reported to have fled into the Congo and Tanzania. Portugal has reportedly increased its armed forces in Angola to more than forty thousand, and in Mozambique to more than twenty thousand. Aircraft and large amounts of transport and matériel have been transferred to the colonies, some of it equipment given Portugal under NATO or purchased from Western sources in consequence of its NATO membership. Such military efforts have imposed an enormous strain on the Portuguese economy, their current costs being estimated at some $100 million annually.

As a result, however, the Angola rebellion seems to have been contained within the northeastern portion of the country, the outbreak of large-scale fighting in Mozambique has been delayed, and nationalist political activity within both areas has become extremely difficult and dangerous. To date, it would appear that the Portuguese attempt to re-establish order and strengthen its control by force has had greater success than the nationalist campaign of sabotage and guerrilla attack.

Within the nationalist movements frustration has been growing, and the more extremist elements of the parties now appear to be increasing their influence. Rival groups, especially the Popular Movement for the Liberation of Angola (MPLA) and the National Democratic Union of Mozambique (UDENAMO), again are challenging the two principal movements. Both Roberto and Mondlane are essentially moderate men who began by rejecting Communist support for their movements. Both have repeatedly sought support from Western and neutral sources, and as a result both have been attacked in Africa as tools of American interests. Although Mondlane has been able to obtain limited American help for purely educational activities, he has failed to obtain other assistance. In disappointment and some bitterness he announced in late 1963 his determination to visit both Moscow and Peking to ask for help. According to unofficial reports, these appeals were successful and FRELIMO was given substantial pledges of both financial and material support.

Early in 1964 Roberto announced that the Angolan nationalists would also accept Communist arms. "Until now we have kept out

of the Cold War and within the framework of African politics,"
he said. "But we are now at a point where a radical change of
policy is imperative for us to make headway in our struggle. . . .
Only the Communists can give us what we need." [7] At the same
time, in a most significant revelation of internal pressures in his
movement, he has agreed to include in his policy council Viriato
da Cruz, regarded as one of the ablest and shrewdest of the Angolan rebel leaders and a dedicated follower of the Peking line.

Thus, as the contest for Angola and Mozambique has come to
focus on military effort, outside factors in steadily widening circles
are being drawn in. The contest may therefore be long as well as
hard, with both sides believing time to be on their side. In esti-
mating the future course of events it is necessary to examine the
likelihood of the staying power of the antagonists.

The Longer and Broader Prospect

Of the Portuguese determination to retain control of the areas
there can be no doubt. Economically they are important. Politically
and psychologically they are perhaps even more important. A living
link with the past, they are also an integral element of Portugal's
pride and self-confidence in being something more than a small
and inconsequential European state.

One cannot assume that the situation in Portugal itself will remain unchanged. Dr. Salazar is an elderly man whose regime is less
than universally popular. If the present level of heavy military out-
lays should have to be continued while earnings from the colonies
decline as a result of disorders, political opposition in Portugal
could become extremely strong. But so far as can be judged, even
if opposition elements should come to power, there is little likelihood of any rapprochement with the African nationalist movements.

On the other hand, Portugal is currently reaping the benefit
of the collapse of central control in the Congo, and of the growing
sense of vulnerability on the part of those newly independent
African states close to the Battleline.

[7] *The New York Times,* January 4, 1964.

The Congo and Tanzania have accorded recognition to the Angolan and Mozambican liberation movements and, far more important, have permitted their territory to be used as bases for military and political operations. But with the advent of Moise Tshombe to power in the Congo and the recurrence of rebellion and secessionist movements there, it is not certain that the Congolese government will give continued backing to the Roberto movement. Chinese support for the rebellion in the eastern provinces of the Congo is not likely to cause Léopoldville to view with enthusiasm the influx of Chinese arms or technicians for use by the Angolan liberation army. Moreover, in view of the increasing danger of Portuguese retaliation and because of the growing vulnerability of the Congo to external pressures, it seems quite possible that the Roberto movement will have less and less opportunity to conduct a political and military campaign against Angola from its Congo base. If that base should be lost, the Angolan rebellion would be set back severely.

The base of the Mozambican movement in Tanzania is not in equal jeopardy. But there are practical limitations to the support and tolerance of revolutionary activity which can be expected from that government. President Nyerere is having some difficulty in holding together his newly united country; his economic situation is tenuous; and his country is highly vulnerable both to retaliatory attack by the Portuguese and to internal political meddling by the Chinese.

The new state of Zambia, flanking Angola and the Congo, has already indicated a keen awareness of the dangers to its own political stability from unrestricted revolutionary activity based on its soil. To judge from statements by Zambian leaders, it is probable that a clear, sharp policy line will be followed, reflecting basic sympathy with the liberation movements but controlling carefully the transit of political refugees and the organization of revolutionary activities within the country.

Malawi is particularly exposed to economic pressures by Portugal through control of the transport through Mozambique of its exports and imports. Malawi's leader, Dr. H. K. Banda, at the meeting of the African states in Cairo in mid-1964, made explicit his unwillingness to participate in any punitive actions against Portugal or its African territories. If Dr. Banda's problems become still more troublesome, and if pressure on Portugal should intensify, they conceivably might agree to discuss a territorial change in the northernmost area of Mozambique which would give Malawi a much-desired outlet to the sea and would provide Portugal with a black buffer state.

In sum, Portugal's holding power in an extended military struggle for Angola and Mozambique is not unlimited. But for the present, and as long as instability or disorder characterizes the neighboring African states, it is possible that Portugal will be able to find ways to prolong control of the areas.

The nationalist movements have marked strengths and weaknesses in any effort to maintain heavy pressure on Angola and Mozambique over an extended period of time. If they can preserve their bases of operation in the Congo and in Tanzania; if they can maintain the solidarity of their political organizations and extend the training and discipline of their military forces; if they can win the active and material support of the OAU; and if they can obtain significant supplies of money and arms from some outside source—then over the longer term their pressure on Portugal should prevail. For not only do they have the moral support of much of the world community, but on purely military grounds, given the great logistical difficulties of Portugal in maintaining defense forces in Africa, they can with each million dollars spent for sabotage and guerrilla attack impose a disproportionately burdensome cost on Portugal in countering their efforts.

Although the OAU has passed resolutions condemning Portugal in the strongest terms and has created a committee to coordinate assistance to the liberation movements, very little effective help has so far reached either the Roberto or the Mondlane forces. It would appear that the OAU, given its many problems, has moved Angola and Mozambique significantly downward in its list of priorities. This appearance may be false, or OAU policy might abruptly change with new political conditions in coming months, but for the present, its intentions and the probable scale of its material support remain unclear.

Similarly, the availability of substantial financial and military assistance from Moscow or Peking is not self-evident. Both the

Russians and the Chinese have declared their readiness to provide money and arms to the revolutionary forces. Still unclear, however, are the willingness of the Congo, Tanzania and the OAU to permit unlimited Communist assistance to flow to the liberation movements, the disposition of the Russians or the Chinese to assume the cost of supporting the revolutionary efforts on the scale and over the time period required for success, and above all, the terms on which such Communist assistance might be forthcoming. With the prevailing uncertainty of their position, frustration, inner splits and public recriminations have increasingly begun to plague the various movements, accompanied by growing pressure from youthful "outs" against more conservative "ins," and incidentally by more expressed hostility to the United States.

Thus, as the struggle for Angola and Mozambique settles down to a protracted test of strength, the outcome increasingly depends on the ability of the antagonists to assemble and hold together political, economic and diplomatic support of progressively broader scope. If the nationalists are able by their efforts to force Portugal to the negotiating table on the key issue of independence, then there may be some prospect for evolutionary change and a degree of stability in the center of Africa. But, if weakness in the liberation movements or growing disorder in independent Africa enables Portugal to thwart political change for several more years, the dangers of eventual and major political explosion may grow worse.

U.N. Actions and the Evolution of U.S. Policy

The diplomatic phase of the battle for the Portuguese territories in Africa has largely been fought at the United Nations; and the evolution of U.S. policy can be traced in its response to the issues raised before the world organization. Portugal became a member of the United Nations in 1955, and shortly thereafter the Secretary-General requested that it submit a list of its "non-self-governing territories." Having changed their designation in 1951 from "colonies" to "provinces," Portugal replied that it did not administer territories of the kind described and declined to provide the information requested on the grounds that affairs in the territories were a matter within the domestic jurisdiction of Portugal. Thereupon began a dispute which smoldered and periodically broke into flame during the following five years as the General Assembly defined with greater specificity the reporting obligations of member states with respect to their overseas territories. In 1960, it went much further, passing a landmark resolution on the colonial question calling for "immediate steps . . . to transfer all powers to the peoples" of dependent territories. Since then, the question of Portugal's African territories has been under almost constant review before the Assembly and other U.N. organs. In a series of resolutions the Assembly has attempted to ameliorate conditions in the areas by call-in upon Portugal to institute various reforms. Other resolutions have urged member governments to use their influence upon Portugal to accept the principle of self-determination and to begin negotiations which would lead the territories toward independence.

Portugal has made a vigorous and skillful defense of its position before the United Nations on legal and diplomatic grounds, steadily insisting that the country is a unitary state and that it is irrelevant to consider the "provinces" in Africa in connection with debates on colonialism. The Portuguese argue that "self-determination" means the right of political participation in the life of a given state, that is to say, Portugal, which the citizens of the African territories already have. They assert that their country is a victim, not the perpetrator, of aggression in Africa. Particularly after India's seizure of Goa in December 1962, they have contended that a double standard of judgment is being applied within the United Nations between the Afro-Asian countries on the one hand and all other states on the other.

The U.S. position, which in the 1950s was in fairly close alignment with that of Portugal, has since become visibly separate and critical. In March 1961, after the Angolan uprisings, the United States supported a draft resolution in the Security Council attacking Portuguese policy there, and Adlai Stevenson, the U.S. delegate, called for advancement toward full self-determination for the people of Angola. Although the resolution was eventually defeated by a combination of European and Latin American abstentions, the significance of the U.S. vote was not lost either on the Africans or on Portugal. As the United States moved further toward outright opposition to Portugal on colonial issues during 1962 and 1963, it pursued a generally unsuccessful attempt to placate both sides, finding itself repeatedly pleading for resolutions which amounted to much less than the majority and rather more than Portugal felt able to accept. By mid-1964, U.S. policy had arrived at the following point, as stated by Deputy Assistant Secretary of State for African Affairs, J. Wayne Fredericks: "We in the United States are deeply committed to self-determination for all people. We believe Portugal should recognize publicly that the principle of self-determination is applicable to its territories. Our policy is to encourage both Portugal and the Africans to come to a workable understanding." [8]

The NATO obligations of the United States and its security interests in the military base on the Azores have played an important role in shaping U.S. policy on the question of the Portuguese territories in Africa. These are separate but related problems, about which there have been some misconceptions. It has sometimes been assumed that the United States is required by its NATO obligations to defend the "territorial integrity" of Portugal, including the African colonies; and that failure to do so would undermine not only relations with Portugal but the whole structure of the alliance. These are erroneous and simplistic formulations which are not useful in evolving a policy taking into account the actual complexities of the situation.

Under the North Atlantic Treaty the United States and the other signatories are obliged "by means of continuous and effective self-help and mutual aid" to "maintain and develop their . . . capacity to resist armed attack" (Article 3). Article 4 specifies that "the Parties will consult together whenever . . . the territorial integrity, political independence or security of any of the Parties is threatened"; and Article 5 states "that an armed attack against one . . . shall be considered an attack against them all." However, "an armed attack . . . is deemed to include an armed attack on the territory of any of the Parties in Europe or North America, on the Algerian departments of France, . . . on the islands under the jurisdiction of any Party in the North Atlantic area north of the Tropic of Cancer . . ." (Article 6). Thus, the treaty clearly

[8] Speech delivered July 7, 1964 at the University of Minnesota, *Department of State Bulletin.*

omits Angola and Mozambique from the territories covered, nor does it in any way bind the signatories to support the colonial policies of other NATO members.

On the practical question of whether support for Portugal on issues involving Angola and Mozambique would have a strengthening effect on the NATO alliance, or whether opposition to Portugal would weaken it, several considerations must be examined. The alliance has developed serious weaknesses in recent years, but these do not relate primarily to differences over colonial policy. They turn on more central issues of strategy, burden-sharing, and nuclear weapons control. Not only is there serious doubt, therefore, that U.S. support for Portugal on African questions would have any visible effect in strengthening NATO, but unequivocal support might measurably weaken the alliance. A majority of the NATO member states have voted against Portugal on key African issues at the United Nations, and some—particularly the Scandinavian countries—have strong views in opposition to Portuguese colonial policy. In addition, the Labour government in Great Britain and Socialist elements in France and the German Federal Republic have generally been unsympathetic to the Salazar regime and would not be more favorably disposed toward NATO if the United States were to identify itself closely with Portuguese policy in Africa.

Indeed, it can fairly be said that in separating itself from Portuguese policy in Africa the United States has not formally violated its treaty obligations nor has it improperly neglected a friend and ally. Having a fundamental difference of view with Portugal, the United States has gone as far as could be realistically expected to consult with Lisbon and to mute the attack against it. The United States has worked for agreed and not imposed solutions.

With respect to the Azores base, the question presented is not one of U.S. obligations under NATO, but rather of balancing broad U.S. interests in Africa as against the direct security values of the base. The Azores base is a facility made available to the United States under a direct arrangement with Portugal, first signed in 1951. Since expiration of the agreement in 1962, the United States has continued to use the facility on a temporary basis while negotiation for an extension of the lease has been carried on. During these protracted discussions the U.S. government has been particularly hesitant to take any steps contrary to Portugal's wishes at the United Nations or elsewhere.

In the view of American military authorities the Azores facility is important for at least three reasons: it provides a staging base for air transport; it has been a refueling base for the U.S. strategic air power; and the naval mission there serves both as a communications center and as the hub of submarine operations in the eastern Atlantic. The Azores base is not generally considered "indispensable" in the sense that its loss would deeply damage American security, although it would impose additional expense and a reduction of flexibility in the base system as a whole.

In looking to the future, the Azores facility is likely to be of diminishing importance as intercontinental missiles are further developed and as longer-range transport and other planes reduce the need for refueling bases. Its long-term value will therefore primarily be in terms of naval requirements.

The United States would like to remain in the Azores as long as it can. On the other hand, in the present judgment of some American defense officials, if a flat choice had to be made between retaining the Azores or retaining U.S. military assets and relationships on the African continent, the latter would take precedence over the former. This is a choice which the United States has not so far had to make and which it would obviously prefer not to have to make.

Within the U.S. government, sharp division appears to continue to exist on issues involving Portugal and the African colonies. In the State and Defense Departments, those mainly concerned with Europe and the NATO alliance have rarely seen eye to eye with those responsible for relations with Africa.

Recommendations for U.S. Policy

In formulating its policy toward the Portuguese areas the United States has been engaged in a difficult process of assessing the facts amid a welter of conflicting claims and assertions, clarifying the legal issues involved, responding to new world conditions and political trends, fulfilling its proper obligations to an allied country, and serving its own short- and long-term national interests. This has not been an easy combination of requirements to satisfy simultaneously.

As to the facts of the situation in Angola and Mozambique, the United States appears to have accepted the findings of a number of U.N. reports and independent investigations that Portuguese administration of the territories has been a clear failure in human terms. Despite Portuguese aims and contentions, the people are notably backward, ignorant, and oppressed.

Similarly on the legal issues which Portugal has raised, the United States seems to concur that developments within the areas are not purely a matter of domestic jurisdiction and that Portugal's international responsibilities include an obligation not only to report on conditions in the territories but to grant self-determination, which in the course of time probably means independence.

Americans have not been untroubled by Portuguese contentions that there is a double standard of values apparent in some of the actions of the United Nations and by Portuguese criticism of a generally emotional and impetuous spirit in its discussions. Measured judgment, however, has brought the United States to the position of favoring self-determination for Angola and Mozambique.

Despite the fact that the struggle has now become primarily a test of the strength of the antagonists, the United States should first of all continue to attempt to influence both Portugal and the nationalist movements toward peaceful change through persuasion and communication, refraining from direct economic or military help to either side. If such diplomatic efforts do not succeed in a reasonable period of time, then it must be recognized that the intensification of fighting and the progressive involvement of Communist arms will cast increasing doubt on the tenability of a policy of refusing material help to both sides.

As part of the effort to exercise its influence, the United States should eliminate certain inconsistencies which now becloud its position and which weaken and confuse its efforts. The statements of American diplomatic representatives in Lisbon, for example, have sometimes served to disquiet and dismay the African states as well as some Europeans. Similarly, programs relating to Angola or Mozambique have sometimes been undertaken by one arm of the U.S. government only to be countermanded by another after various hopes and expectations had been raised among the nationalists.

American spokesmen have said that there is no necessary inconsistency between the official objectives of strengthening NATO and of promoting African independence. But there is profound inconsistency in an American policy which attempts to preserve stability in Africa, to persuade the Portuguese to make fundamental political concessions in Angola and Mozambique, and at the same time allows Portugal the benefit of substantial American financial and military aid in maintaining physical control of those areas. Unless and until effective measures can be devised to prevent any further use by Portugal of NATO and American arms in Africa, all U.S. diplomatic efforts of persuasion will be deeply undercut.

As a second aspect of its policy, it would be highly desirable for the United States to regain a degree of flexibility and maneuverability in its dealings with Lisbon on the Azores base problem by preparing some military alternatives to that base. Thus, a serious move to begin the gradual transfer of some U.S. operations from the Azores to other Atlantic installations might have a most useful effect upon all diplomatic dealings with Portugal. Nor would the result of such initiative necessarily mean the loss of the Azores base to the United States and to NATO. If the United States could regain a negotiating posture, it might well discover that Portugal would go to considerable lengths not to lose the several advantages of an American presence on the islands.

Third, it is urgent that the United States, while maintaining diplomatic relationships with Portugal, substantially strengthen its communication and contact with the nationalist movements, which may well be the actual governments of Angola and Mozambique within a few years. If the United States hopes to have some basis of friendly relationship with them, it should promptly and substantially increase its efforts both in relief assistance and educational assistance. Such help in existing circumstances can best be carried out through responsible private organizations in the United States and elsewhere. Certain projects could be best executed on an international basis and in cooperation with some of the independent African states.

At the present time Russian and Chinese programs for the training of agitators, saboteurs, and military personnel from southern Africa are several times as great as refugee education projects of the United States. In confining its assistance to educational rather than military and political training the United States is already taking a calculated risk; and if the problems in Angola and Mozambique enter a totally military phase, then the type of training now being offered by the Russians and the Chinese will give their "graduates" particular prominence and importance in the guerrilla and civil wars to come. Nevertheless, as of now it is both prudent and reasonably promising for the United States to confine its efforts to the educational field, provided those efforts are increased in scale.

Fourth, the United States should make a new and more vigorous attempt through the United Nations or otherwise to initiate measures and programs to prepare Angola and Mozambique for self-government. If these areas, at the present time so backward in every respect, were suddenly by some combination of circumstances to achieve independence, a situation even more chaotic than that of the Congo could well ensue.

In addition to greatly expanded educational programs offered to political refugees from the two territories, it would be useful if the United States, directly or in combination with African and European states, could work with Portugal and the nationalist movements to step up training for qualified younger persons in Angola and Mozambique, particularly at the secondary and technical level. There is an inherent instability, almost danger, in any kind of political change in the areas while the number of trained Africans is as shockingly inadequate as at present. One clear lesson of the Congo is that political change can come suddenly; and its consequences can be disastrous if major and timely steps are not taken to prepare a cadre of qualified and capable indigenous leaders.

Continuation of the present course of U.S. policy, as modified by the above recommendations, may offer some hopeful prospects, particularly if the United States can combine its influence with that of the United Kingdom and perhaps France and Spain. Although the Portuguese government has repeatedly stated its refusal to modify its position on self-determination, its policy has in fact significantly changed under the pressure of criticism and world opinion in recent years. Faced with greater firmness by the United States and other Western powers with close ties to Portugal in support of further policy changes, it is not impossible that the Salazar government would make them. Similarly, among the African nationalists an increasing spirit of realism prevails as their difficulties multiply. If the United States and others can succeed in bringing about some progressive modification of Portuguese policy, this might well be sufficient to restrain the more extreme and dangerous tendencies on the African side.

The stakes in the game are considerable. The course recommended involves risks, but the present impasse presents serious risks also. The success to date of Portuguese military efforts in repressing rebellion and the current disarray of the nationalist movements mean nothing more than a pause in the broad political process at work. If an intensification of pressure upon Portugal opens a path to negotiations for self-government, then two eventualties can be anticipated. First, the concrete proposals which emerge are likely to be complex and imperfect compromises. But the United States should be prepared to react to them in flexible and pragmatic fashion. If they represent agreement between the political forces involved, and if they mean movement in the general political direction of self-government, then doctrinaire tests of principle should not be applied. Second, if two more independent, or relatively independent, African states should take form in Angola and Mozambique as a result of negotiations, disorder and dispute may be expected to accompany and to follow their birth. But such hazards must be weighed against the even greater dangers of long-term instability and Communist penetration which will grow from a prolongation of the present pattern of Portuguese intransigence.

The urgency of intensifying pressures for negotiations derives from the fact that if some serious political evolution is not engendered in Angola and Mozambique within the coming two or three years, the United States will likely face far more dangerous and painful choices than at present.

Chapter III

Rhodesia

Rhodesia * is a vivid illustration of the diversity of the situations in southern Africa, despite the prevalence of white political control. If Angola and Mozambique now suggest the possibility of stalemate, of blocking the southward advance of black nationalism, Rhodesia suggests the possibility of sudden and drastic change. If Portugal represents a metropole determined to hold its colonies at all costs, Britain represents a metropole ready, even eager, to disengage from Rhodesia, if only some honorable and reasonable basis for withdrawal can be found.

And if the political situations in Angola, Mozambique and South Africa present studies in absolutes, Rhodesia is a portrait in shadings of gray. It is a test case of the ability of the world community, by means of external economic and political influence, to guide the internal constitutional development of a country; of the ability of the whites of the area effectively to resist external and internal pressures to relinquish their control; and of the ability of black nationalist leaders to mount those pressures. In a still more profound sense Rhodesia is a test case of the ability of men of different races in the passionate political atmosphere of southern Africa today to find a peaceful basis for living together within the same national frontiers.

Rhodesia is a landlocked country, interposed between the African and the white-controlled governments of the continent. Its population totals some 3.8 million, of whom less than 200,000

* In October 1964, with the independence of Northern Rhodesia and the change of its name to Zambia, Southern Rhodesia changed its name to Rhodesia.

are Europeans. Although a spacious country of good climate, Rhodesia is not rich. Economically, politically and strategically it is a dependent area. Independent Zambia, to the north, is not only a source of much of the rail traffic which passes through Rhodesia, but also an important market for Rhodesia's products. Mozambique, on the east, controls the outlets of Rhodesia's railroads to the Indian Ocean. South Africa is a vital market, and increasingly a source of political comfort and economic support to the embattled Rhodesian whites. Great Britain, in addition to its tenuous but important political link with Rhodesia, has great economic influence because it is the principal buyer of Rhodesian products, particularly tobacco, the country's main export.

In recent years the Rhodesian situation has been alternately quiescent and tense. But now, as new forces gather within and outside the country, it appears to be approaching a climax. The conflict between two different traditions of British colonial policy—Britain's imperial interests and those of its colonial settlers on the one hand, and its responsibilities as trustee for the native peoples on the other—is epitomized in Rhodesia, the legatee of both.

The Drift Toward Conflict

Its modern history began when David Livingstone arrived in 1855 at Victoria Falls. The discovery of gold in Mashonaland, now part of Rhodesia, in the 1860s attracted Cecil Rhodes and brought white settlers into the area. In 1889 Rhodes' British South Africa Company was given a charter with exclusive rights to occupy for trading and mining all the territory from Bechuanaland to the Zambezi and ultimately up to Lake Tanganyika. Four years later the name Rhodesia was first proclaimed for the territory. The establishment of British hegemony had to be accomplished against the active opposition of local African tribes. The principal of these, the Matabele and the Mashona, conducted a series of violent uprisings, the last of which in 1897 was so totally repressed that the native ruling class was virtually annihilated.

Under its charter the British South Africa Company governed the territory, exercising quasi-sovereign powers. The charter, however, clearly reserved to the British government the role of overseer, particularly in regard to the welfare of the Africans. A later Order in Council of 1898 contained the following native rights clause: "No conditions, disabilities or restrictions shall, without the previous consent of the Secretary of State, be imposed upon the natives by ordinances which do not equally apply to persons of European descent, save in the supply of arms, ammunition and liquor."

In 1922, as the expiration date of the British South Africa Company's charter approached, the white settlers in the area then known as Southern Rhodesia were given the opportunity to choose by referendum between joining the Union of South Africa or being granted responsible government as a British colony. Eighty-eight hundred voted to draft a constitution for self-government against six thousand who voted to join the Union on generous terms offered by General Smuts. Thus, by decision of less than three thousand whites, Southern Rhodesia in 1923 became a self-governing colony of the British Crown. The composition of its all-white parliament was not significantly altered for the next forty years.

Under the 1923 constitution, though it contained a restatement of the earlier native rights clause and reserved to London a right of review over legislation, Southern Rhodesia was free of effective British control of its domestic policy. Its legislature of white members was elected by an almost entirely white electorate. It provided limited educational opportunity to the Africans, largely through subsidized missionary schools. It was not a racist society in the most brutal sense, but it clearly relegated the African to an inferior economic, political, social, and educational position.

The vast area originally embraced by the British South Africa Company's charter in the course of time had developed into three political units, Northern Rhodesia, Nyasaland and Southern Rhodesia, the first two being directly ruled British colonies with very few whites in their population. In the late 1940s white sentiment in all three favored joining them in a new political federation. From a white Southern Rhodesian viewpoint the advantages in such a step were largely economic, principally an expanded market for its products, a share of the rich tax revenues from copper production in Northern Rhodesia, and a shifting to the federal government of its heavy public debt. When federation materialized under the leadership of Sir Roy Welensky, it did in fact bring these hoped-for advantages to Southern Rhodesia.

The motives of the whites of the three territories, however, were not solely economic. Some of them saw in federation a means of lessening the influence of the Colonial Office in London over native affairs, an influence which they regarded as too favorable to the African. The Labour government then in power had asserted Britain's "special responsibility to the African communities" and pledged that "full account would have to be taken of African opinion before any constitutional change affecting African interests could be considered." [1] Yet the first Federal Prime Minister, Sir Godfrey Huggins, said shortly after the inception of the Federation in 1953 that he "had no doubt it would be quite easy to get rid of the reservations which the Federal Constitution would have regarding African rights." [2]

The Federation came to be such a symbol of white domination that it served to arouse and focus African nationalist sentiment. During the ten years of its lifetime nationalist activity was intensified, and political demands became more urgent. Fear fed upon fear, and by 1959 a state of emergency had developed in much of Central Africa. To study the disquieting and deteriorating situation the British government created the Monckton Commission, which reported in 1960 that African opposition to the Federation was "almost pathological." Consequently the Commission recommended changes in the federal constitution including a parity of seats for Africans and Europeans in parliament. It also recommended that Northern Rhodesia and Nyasaland be given the right to secede. This recommendation launched a disintegration process which culminated in late 1962 with the British decision that Nyasaland would be allowed to withdraw. A similar announcement was made in March 1963 with respect to Northern Rhodesia.

Although the Federation did not formally disappear until December 31, 1963, it had clearly become unhinged by late 1960. In the atmosphere of concern which then prevailed, Duncan Sandys, Secretary for Commonwealth Relations, was able to persuade Sir

[1] Statement of the Colonial Secretary, Arthur Creech Jones. House of Commons, *Parliamentary Debates* (1948–49), v. 461, p. 292.

[2] *Rhodesia Herald*, April 3, 1953.

Edgar Whitehead, the Prime Minister of Southern Rhodesia, to agree to constitutional talks. Out of these came the first fundamental change in Southern Rhodesia's constitution in forty years, including provision for the first African participation in its parliament in the colony's history. Under the revised constitution fifteen out of the sixty-five seats were in effect reserved for African representatives. The constitution committed Southern Rhodesia to work toward a fully democratic system of government in which the will of the majority eventually would prevail.

In its wording the revised document, known as the Sandys constitution, set forth a philosophy of political gradualism and the progressive advent of the African to political power as he acquired more education and economic status. Whether the concessions made to African political aspirations were *bona fide* or were merely a carefully contrived device to preserve white political control was a matter on which opinion was sharply divided. In a referendum held in 1961 the white electorate approved the new constitution by a vote of 2 to 1. The then governing United Federal Party hailed the outcome as a sign that Southern Rhodesian Europeans genuinely favored sharing political power with the Africans and ending racial discrimination.

In fact, however, the motivation of the white voters and the meaning of their endorsement were complex to analyze. For some the vote reflected a serious desire to find a new path of political partnership with the Africans and a reasonable evolutionary solution to the deep racial divisions. Others, however, in endorsing "eventual" political control by the African had in mind an indefinite and very protracted span of years. For still others the new constitution, despite its wording, provided new opportunities for insuring white political control. It transferred Britain's reserved powers over Southern Rhodesian legislation to a new Constitutional Council and further stipulated that an adverse ruling on a bill by the Council could be overridden by a simple repassage in the Legislative Assembly. Moreover, the Declaration of Rights in the new constitution did not apply to pre-existing discriminatory laws, including the crucial Land Apportionment Act and a variety of security legislation aimed at the Africans—and in any event it could be suspended during periods of "public emergency."

The new constitution gave a momentary fillip to hopes that the deteriorating racial situation within the country could be improved. But these were soon extinguished in a rapidly growing environment of fear and frustration. From the point of view of the whites, events within the country and outside were rushing headlong toward black nationalist domination. Violence in Nyasaland had created a state of panic among the whites. In Northern Rhodesia Kenneth Kaunda's United National Independence Party was forcefully and dramatically consolidating its power. One after another, the newly independent African states to the north appeared to be sliding toward one-party control and anti-white militancy. Katanga's secession had added to the disorder in the Congo, and rebellion continued in Angola.

In the first election held under the new constitution in December 1962, which was boycotted by the blacks, the white electorate voted out the relatively moderate government of Sir Edgar Whitehead and put into power a more intransigent group under Winston J. Field as Prime Minister. The Whitehead regime had represented the older establishment, with strong sentimental ties to Britain and loyalty to the Crown. It had maintained discriminatory practices of many kinds—but it had also removed some and had always spoken in terms consistent with British parliamentary tradition. Indeed, in the election campaign of 1962 Sir Edgar's party sounded almost liberal, favoring the repeal of discriminatory legislation and indicating the possibility of an African majority in the legislature within fifteen years.

The Rhodesian Front under Winston Field, on the other hand, reflected the outlook of the white farmers and artisans. It denounced concessions to the Africans and openly asserted the indispensability of white political control. It stressed the idea of Rhodesian independence and of cutting ties with "untrustworthy" Britain, a theme which was to assume greater importance in the months following. Its advent reflected a degree of concern and determination on the part of the majority of whites which was unprecedented—including a readiness to resort to desperate measures.

The attitudes of the Africans of Southern Rhodesia in rejecting the new constitution and boycotting the elections of 1962 were as complex and as fear-ridden as those of the whites. Events over several years prior to the elections had produced among African nationalists first disappointment, then skepticism, and finally great bitterness toward the whites. At the same time, events elsewhere in Africa served to increase their hopes of an early political victory and their unwillingness to accept the political concessions of the new constitution as adequate.

Political currents within the country were already moving in contradictory directions under Sir Edgar Whitehead's government. After 1962 the gap widened, the blacks becoming more impatient in their demands and the whites increasingly reluctant to offer even the qualified concessions of the new constitution. The political struggle has therefore become not that of African and white political parties operating within a constitutional framework but rather a struggle for power on a racial basis. Communication and confidence between racial groups have largely broken down, repression has increased, and the spiraling descent toward crisis has become more precipitate.

When the ill-fated Federation finally broke up at the end of 1963, Nyasaland and Northern Rhodesia became, in due course, the independent nations of Malawi and Zambia. With the dissolution of the Federation, important economic, administrative, military and other matters had to be rearranged. The consequences were of particular interest to Southern Rhodesia, which in many ways had been the principal beneficiary as well as the predominant partner. Economically the impact was immediately noticeable. Southern Rhodesia lost privileged markets and the benefit it had derived from sharing in the tax revenues of Northern Rhodesia. At the same time it had to resume responsibility for a considerable portion of the large public debt of the Federation. Exports dropped, unemployment increased, and a general mood of depression developed. Considerable numbers of whites emigrated, the influx of capital declined, and important enterprises moved elsewhere.

It is noteworthy, especially in relation to arguments concerning the political effects of proposed sanctions against South Africa, that the pressures of economic difficulty in 1963 and early 1964 in Southern Rhodesia did not move the whites to seek political compromise with the forces of African nationalism. On the contrary, they turned to more reactionary leaders and stiffened their resistance.

Thus, in early 1964 at the bottom of the slump, the Rhodesian Front government moved toward taking the drastic step of independence from Britain as the only feasible solution to continued political and economic uncertainty. In April, Field resigned under pressure and mounting criticism of his leadership by militant rightists in his party. Ian D. Smith, his successor, promptly reorganized the cabinet, bringing in several new ministers sympathetic to his views. He ordered the arrest of the African nationalist leader, Joshua Nkomo, along with several of his chief lieutenants on charges of stirring up violence and intimidation, which led to protests and unrest throughout the African population. By early 1965 it was estimated that some 2,000 Africans were being held in political detention.

In its public statements the Smith government has carefully phrased its goals in the language of the Sandys constitution. Officially, it is committed to "work toward a fully democratic system of government in which the will of the majority will prevail." It emphasizes the need for gradualism, insisting that until the majority can satisfy the qualifications of intelligent, informed participation in public life there will have to be "minority government." It sees the alternatives as "orderly evolution toward a liberal democracy," on the one hand, and "the premature introduction of universal suffrage and the rapid collapse of the democratic structure of the country and its economy," on the other.[3]

In less formal declarations, however, Smith has indicated that he does not believe there will be an African nationalist government in Rhodesia in his lifetime. Such a government, he has stated, would mean the end of European civilization in Southern Rhodesia.[4] Many persons believe that the real interest of his government in seeking independence is to free itself totally from the inhibition of even vestigial British control in order that the Rhodesian whites can direct the affairs of the country as they see fit. "We shall try desperately to gain [independence] by negotiation," Smith has said, "in keeping with the contract we made with the British government at the time of the 1961 referendum. But we reserve the right in the

[3] *The Situation in Southern Rhodesia*, a statement by the Southern Rhodesian government, June 1964, p. 5.
[4] *Rhodesia Herald*, April 17, 1964, reporting press conference of April 16, 1964.

event of other parties to the agreement reneging on their promises
. . . to take matters into our own hands." [5]

Throughout 1964 Smith expressed his demands in the most urgent and absolute terms. Repeatedly he challenged Britain to concede independence and accompanied his challenges with thinly veiled threats of unilateral action. Within Southern Rhodesia his declarations aroused deep misgivings on the part of white opposition elements, who publicly declared their loyalty to the Crown and announced their refusal to accept the authority of any "treasonable" government. London responded warily and diplomatically to Smith's challenges, but without conceding him any ground.

In July of that year a period of dangerous tension arose when Smith was not invited to attend the Commonwealth Prime Minister's conference, a courtesy which had been extended to Southern Rhodesia for thirty years. The impact in Southern Rhodesia was strong. Then, at the conclusion of the meeting the prime ministers issued a pointed statement urging that since the United Kingdom had primary responsibility for Rhodesia's constitutional affairs, it should call a representative conference of Southern Rhodesians—black and white—to decide on terms for the colony's independence.

In September a second moment of possible rupture arrived. Britain's Conservative government, however, was most eager to avoid any development in Southern Rhodesia which could embarrass it in the weeks immediately preceding the British general elections. In that advantageous atmosphere Smith flew to London for talks. But the communiqué which followed several days of argument was a careful compromise.

Smith had conceded in London that the whole population of Rhodesia had a right to be consulted about independence; but in Salisbury he continued to insist on a strictly limited franchise for African voters in running the affairs of the country. In London his demand was for independence "on the basis of the 1961 Constitution," which envisages a progressive take-over of political control by the Africans; but in Salisbury his government continued to imprison African nationalists and block any African political advance. Moreover, it was widely believed that the clear intention of

[5] *Southern Rhodesia News Review,* June 1964.

Smith's party was to rewrite the constitution immediately after independence, eliminating all trace of the political gradualism which
is its distinguishing characteristic. But such obscurity and contra-
diction have seldom been an impediment to political popularity,
and the Rhodesian whites welcomed Smith home as a hero after his
London talks.

Something of the intent of his government could be deduced
from the manner in which Smith subsequently chose to "consult"
the Rhodesian population on the matter of independence. White
opinion would be determined by referendum; but African opinion
would be tested by an "indaba" with the five hundred traditional
chiefs and headmen of the rural native reserves, who were promised
at the same time new increases in chiefs' wages and sweeping new
powers, such as the right to distribute land. The Smith government
completed preparations for its "consultations" during October 1964
and expressed the hope of independence by Christmas. The Rhodesian Front was driving hard to free the country of all British
constitutional control; and the British government continued its
attempt to meet the challenge by deferral, evasiveness and in-
decision.

Then, suddenly, the atmosphere changed when the British electorate on October 15 turned out the Conservatives and brought a
new Labour government to power. Despite a thin margin in the
House of Commons, it moved quickly and forcefully on a number
of key issues—and on none more so than that of Rhodesia. One of
Prime Minister Wilson's first steps was to name as head of the
British Mission to the United Nations, Sir Hugh Foot, who had
resigned in 1962 as representative to the Trusteeship Council in
protest against his government's unwillingness to act more forcefully on the Rhodesian question. Then Wilson, in a letter to Smith,
made clear the severe consequences to Rhodesia of a unilateral
declaration of independence, which would be regarded by Britain
as an "open act of defiance and rebellion." [6] The new Secretary of
State for Commonwealth Relations, Arthur Bottomley, appealed
directly to Rhodesian voters to repudiate Prime Minister Smith
and to force him to resign.[7]

[6] British Information Services release, October 29, 1964.
[7] *The New York Times,* October 28, 1964.

In Smith's referendum the white voters endorsed his independence proposals by an overwhelming majority, and the tribal leaders gave him their unanimous support. But British response was curt and clear: the chiefs' "indaba" could not be considered as representative of the African electorate. In early 1965, however, the Wilson government seemed to lose its confidence and readiness for a showdown, and its conduct became markedly more conciliatory. Yet Smith seemed to be moving relentlessly toward a unilateral declaration of independence, calling for new elections preparatory to making "essential changes" in the constitution. He busily attempted to line up the support of South Africa, Portugal and others to protect Rhodesia from the predictable consequences.

The Coming Contest for Rhodesia

On its surface the Rhodesian political struggle is an African paradox: the whites, not the blacks, are asserting their right to independence and denouncing the intrusion of a Western power. And the blacks, far from favoring independence, are insisting upon the intervention of Great Britain for a new political solution.

On closer examination, however, the situation is not as upside-down as it would seem. Independence is seen by the Rhodesian whites as their best hope for maintaining control; while for the blacks Britain's continuing presence is their best hope for forcing the whites to accept the principle of majority rule. For Britain the careful use of its limited powers is its best hope in fulfilling a complex set of responsibilities and moderating political tension.

For the Rhodesian government the drive for independence and its threatened recourse to a unilateral declaration represents a gamble of major proportions. How strongly and steadfastly will it be able to hold to this risky course and its consequences? From many points of view Rhodesia and the Smith government seem to be in a vulnerable position.

In simple population terms less than 200,000 Rhodesian whites are not likely to have great staying power against the pressures of 3,600,000 blacks. Economically, Rhodesia is neither strong nor self-sufficient. Although its mining, manufacturing and agriculture have prospered, the country is dependent on outside sources for both capital and markets. Unlike the South African economy, for example, Rhodesia's ability to survive in an adverse international economic climate is sharply limited.

Militarily, Rhodesia has the equipment necessary to deal with internal disorder and to repulse Zambia or Malawi if they should intervene. After the breakup of the Federation, Rhodesia reacquired control of the bulk of its military resources, including one European battalion, one African battalion, a parachute commando squadron, and most of the jet-equipped Royal Rhodesian Air Force. These forces, however, would not necessarily be available to the government in the event of a unilateral declaration of independence. Their commander-in-chief is the Crown-appointed governor, and the members of the armed forces have sworn their loyalty to the Crown. In the event of an unconstitutional action the governor would presumably be obliged to take his instructions from London, not Salisbury, and to arrest those disobeying his orders, including not only members of the armed forces but also the officials of a rebellious government.

Diplomatically, too, Rhodesia has few sources of powerful support to draw upon. Portugal, though possibly sympathetic with certain views of the present Rhodesian government, has cautioned Prime Minister Smith against the hazards of unilateral independence and continues to maintain an aloof position. South Africa has offered certain economic assistance and has warned Britain against direct interference. But the extent to which Rhodesia and South Africa will be willing to move toward a mutual defense agreement or political merger remains unclear. Thus, if it unilaterally declares independence, Rhodesia might well find itself virtually as isolated in the world community as South Africa, and far less able to resist the consequent international pressures.

Perhaps the greatest contrast between the situations in Rhodesia and South Africa lies in the former's lack of a hard core of able and unified white leaders, of a formulated ideology such as apartheid to guide government policy, and of a firm and cohesive body of white support behind the government. Despite increasing support for the Smith government, white opposition is still present and long-established habits of racial moderation, respect for constitutionality, and identification with Great Britain impose major obstacles to the type of authoritarianism and exploitation practiced in South Africa. The Rhodesian courts still do not hesitate to strike down as illegal various repressive actions of the government. The members of Sir Edgar Whitehead's party do not hesitate to declare their loyalty to the Crown, and eloquent statements of dissent are still heard from individual members of the white community.

The white community as a whole gives the impression of human beings distressed, bewildered, caught in a riptide of political events. In their anxiety they seem now to have turned toward solutions of resistance, not accommodation, and to give their support increasingly to leaders who speak in simple, unequivocal and aggressive tones. For many, however, their new affiliation is tentative and unenthusiastic; and in the event of a rupture of relations with Britain or of widespread brutality or bloodshed, significant shifts of white attitudes could still occur.

To offset the many elements of weakness in their position, Prime Minister Smith and his colleagues count on at least three fundamental assets. First, as long as the Rhodesian government can maintain itself in power and preserve a reasonable degree of civil order it is extremely unlikely that Britain, with its restricted powers of intervention, would attempt unilaterally to impose a new constitution. Second, while ugly disorders continue in the independent nations of Africa the moral position of the African states in criticizing Rhodesia is undercut, and the sympathy of the Western countries for the predicament of the Rhodesian whites is re-enforced. Third and most important, the African population of Rhodesia is to a large extent politically inert, poorly led, and divided.

Since World War II, and as an accompaniment to Rhodesian economic development, many Africans have been drawn toward the cities and into industrial employment. But the large majority still live in the tribal areas, gaining a meager existence on remote farms. There the chiefs and headmen retain considerable influence, though in political terms they are of little consequence. Poorly educated and backward-looking, they have played no leadership role in the issues which have stirred the African community in recent years, and neither in their persons nor their position do they hold the respect of the African population.

The African nationalist leaders have been most active among the detribalized urban Africans, though they have also been making headway in the tribal areas, particularly among younger people. African political sentiment in the contemporary sense remained largely unorganized until the late 1950s when the African National Congress was reactivated under the leadership of Joshua Nkomo. With increasing effectiveness it began to challenge the political monopoly of Rhodesia's whites, and in 1959 it was banned. Each of its subsequent incarnations under varying names has met a similar fate. The high point of nationalist effectiveness was reached in 1960 and 1961 when under unified leadership the movement was able to exert strong and constructive influence on the constitutional conferences held in London and Salisbury in those years. Since then, however, it has suffered considerable losses both in its effectiveness and in its unity.

To an important degree this weakness is explainable by the severe repressive measures of the Rhodesian government against African political activity. Key African leaders have been restricted, imprisoned, or driven into self-exile. Their organizations have been harassed and forced underground. However, the decline in influence of the nationalist movement may have been due in part to the low quality of its leadership and to fundamental errors of judgment on crucial occasions. In 1963 the Reverend Ndabaningi Sithole and most of the intellectuals in Nkomo's party broke away to form a new group. Charging Nkomo with "unwarrantable political inactivity," they sought to break his hold on the rank and file of his movement. They did succeed in penetrating the African labor movement and in making other limited gains. But Nkomo was able to hold the bulk of his popular support and to maintain the endorsement of important African leaders outside the country. More recently, tribalism for the first time appears to be entering as a divisive factor, and personal rivalries for power have reached a dangerous point of acrimony and obstinacy.

Were the African nationalists to unite, and particularly if able younger leaders were to emerge, then all calculations—including those of the Smith government—regarding the political future would have to be revised. But as the situation stands, disunity, mediocrity and inactivity in the Rhodesian nationalist forces is one of the principal assets on which the government can count.

On the whole, however, in any confrontation with Britain the government would seem to have more weaknesses than strength. Though capable of rallying the whites within the country around a negative program of resistance, it has been incapable of attracting powerful allies abroad. It seems too weak to repress black nationalism over any considerable period of time, but not too weak in its desperation to hazard a drastic and damaging unilateral action. Such action might well bring down upon Rhodesia crushing forces from outside and thus cause the very thing which the white leaders hope to avoid, namely a new constitution imposed by Britain and a government controlled by the African majority.

Several outside influences play upon the Rhodesian situation to the advantage of the African nationalist cause, but on the whole these are likely to be of only secondary importance. Zambia and Malawi, by their location and the fact of their sympathy with the African nationalists, will provide a safe haven for refugees and political exiles; and Zambia under certain circumstances might provide a base of operation for a Rhodesian nationalist government-in-exile. But because Zambia and Malawi are dependent on rail traffic through Rhodesia and are vulnerable to powerful retaliatory steps which Rhodesia might take, they are likely to be moderating influences in the councils of the independent African states rather than sources of active pressure against Rhodesia.

The Organization of African Unity, at its 1963 meeting in Addis Ababa, expressed concern about the Rhodesian situation; but because of the intervention of some of the more moderate African leaders, Rhodesia was not given the priority accorded to Angola and South Africa. At the 1964 meeting in Lagos, however, a shift in attitude became apparent when the OAU resolved that member states "consider their diplomatic and other relations with Britain should the British government ignore" their recommendation to "prevent effectively the threat of unilateral independence or subtle assumption of power by the minority settler regime in Southern Rhodesia. . . ." At its meeting of heads of states in Cairo in July 1964 the OAU had come to consider Rhodesia one of its "primary targets," more urgent perhaps even than Angola and Mozambique. Following the Cairo meeting the OAU urged consideration of economic and diplomatic boycotts against Rhodesia.

The ability of the OAU to impose effective sanctions or to exert forceful pressure on Rhodesia is handicapped by the same problems which obstruct its efforts in other southern African situations—disunity, lack of resources, organizational weakness, a lack of conviction on the part of some member states, and the restraining influence of those located on the southern African periphery. In the short term, the OAU will be a continuing source of inflammatory statements, but its actual influence is not likely to be great.

Similarly, although both the Russian and the Chinese Communists have expressed interest in Rhodesia's "liberation," neither has yet been willing to make a major commitment of resources to it. The Chinese are reported to have courted certain African nationalist leaders, and both Russia and China are believed to have given numerous training grants to young Rhodesian political refugees. But because of restrictions upon nationalist activity, the lack of an organized Communist movement within the country, and the absence of a Rhodesian "liberation army" outside, neither Russia nor China has yet been able to establish a foothold.

In the United Nations the Rhodesian question has been of increasing prominence since 1961, when the General Assembly affirmed over British objections that Southern Rhodesia was a non-self-governing territory. Since then the Assembly has maintained pressure through passing resolutions calling, *inter alia,* for a new constitutional conference with the participation of all parties concerned on a one-man-one-vote basis; the release of nationalist leaders, an end to the ban on their organizations, and restoration of rights to non-Europeans; and refusal by Britain of the "settler minority government" demand for independence. In September 1963 Britain vetoed a Security Council resolution calling upon it not to transfer the armed forces of the defunct federation to Southern Rhodesia and not to transfer any powers or attributes of sovereignty until the establishment of a government fully representative of all inhabitants.

What moral or persuasive influence resolutions adopted by the OAU or sponsored by the Afro-Asian bloc in the United Nations will have in the future depends in part, of course, on the general pattern of conduct of these states on the international scene. But without question the single, overwhelmingly most important external influence which will affect the political future of Rhodesia is that of the British government itself.

The Role of Great Britain

The powers and instruments which Britain has available to deal with the Rhodesian problem are legal, military, economic, diplomatic, sentimental, and traditional. Rhodesia, while it enjoys internal self-government, is not an independent member of the Commonwealth. Though by convention the British Parliament will not legislate on any matter within the competence of the Rhodesian Parliament, the British government under the present constitution has the power to disallow legislation inconsistent with the Crown's international responsibilities. And there are limitations upon Rhodesia's power to amend its constitution where the powers of the governor and the place of the Crown in the constitution are concerned.

The limitations on Rhodesia's independence cannot legally be removed unilaterally. Unless British cooperation and consent are given, independence for Rhodesia could not be obtained by constitutional means. In the event that Rhodesia should take unconstitutional action in the form of a unilateral declaration of independence, Britain, in theory, would have full right to intervene. Constitutionally, such a situation would release it from the obligations imposed by convention not to legislate for Rhodesia. The present constitution thus could be suspended. In the event of rebellion the governor and the courts could disregard any resolution of the Legislative Assembly and could dissolve the Assembly itself if necessary, exercising temporary legislative power and taking over the executive responsibility of government. British subjects in Rhodesia might be subject to the sanction of English criminal law and could be charged with treasonable acts if they supported the rebellion.

In addition, the British government could bring to bear on Rhodesia powerful economic pressures. It could forbid all transfers into or out of Rhodesian sterling accounts in the United Kingdom; it could freeze private accounts with commercial banks as well as the central banking reserves of Rhodesia which are kept in London.

Britain could also withdraw the guarantees on behalf of Rhodesia which it has given to the World Bank. Perhaps the heaviest economic sanction which Britain could impose would be denial to Rhodesia of Commonwealth preference on its tobacco. This would mean a heavy blow to Rhodesian export earnings since tobacco produces nearly 40 per cent of its foreign exchange, and British manufacturers buy approximately one hundred million pounds of Rhodesian tobacco every season. Other exports such as beef, asbestos and sugar, which enjoy a small preference or quotas, might similarly be affected. Finally, if Rhodesia were to be deprived of the privileges of Commonwealth membership, numerous advantages in the sphere of technical advice, assistance and cooperation would be lost.

To what extent Britain would actually exert the available legal and other pressures upon Rhodesia remains to be seen. Until the advent of the present Labour government London showed great reluctance to deal with the territory other than on the basis of consultation, negotiation and voluntary agreement. Prime Minister Wilson, as we have seen, responded to Ian Smith's defiance with the warning that any declaration of independence would be an open act of rebellion. In his October 27 statement, Commonwealth Secretary Bottomley indicated that the first retaliatory moves by Britain would be economic, and that Britain would regard it as treasonable if British companies should continue to invest in Rhodesia under such circumstances. At the same time, however, he said that the use of armed intervention was not being considered.

For Britain, the choices are complex and painful. The British government has not only sentimental and traditional ties with the white residents of Rhodesia but moral obligations to them as well, having strongly encouraged their settlement of the area in the past. Moreover, in considering action against Rhodesia the British government must pay heed to British public opinion—which is generally sympathetic to the whites. A public opinion poll taken on the basis of a nationwide sample in Britain in the summer of 1964 produced the following results:

> "If Southern Rhodesia declares itself to be independent without being granted independence by Britain, which of the following steps do you think the British government should take?"

Send in troops to put down rebellion—6%
Recognize Rhodesia as fully independent—43%
Neither recognize nor send in troops—19.5%
Don't know—31.5%

"In these circumstances [unilateral independence] do you think Britain should or should not apply economic sanctions against Southern Rhodesia?"

Should—12%
Should not—44%
Don't know—44% [8]

Such evidence suggests that the British government is caught in a web of relationships and obligations not only in Rhodesia and with regard to the world community, but also with its own electorate. In the past these complexities have produced a softness and tardiness of action on the part of Great Britain. The new Wilson government, having encountered early political reverses at home and increasingly severe economic problems, may not persist in its initial vigorous approach to the Rhodesian question. In that event, a return to the former policy of "muddling through" may occur.

However, if the Labour government holds to its earlier declarations of intent, then Britain's potential power and authority in the situation should bring home to Smith and his government, if they have any reasonable sense of prudence or practicality, the great risks of unilateral action. But even if unilateral independence is deterred, the more complicated question remains whether Britain will be able to check and reverse the spiral toward racial violence in Rhodesia which is now under way. For although Britain may have substantial powers and strong impulse to deal with a specific and treasonable action by Rhodesia, it has fewer clear powers and probably less impulse to vigorous action in dealing with a sustained and technically legal effort by the Rhodesian whites to maintain their power. Moreover, the racial situation has now so deteriorated that it is difficult to conceive what a constructive solution might be.

Looking back on those crucial years when attitudes in Rhodesia hardened into the lines in which they are drawn today, Sir Hugh

[8] National Opinion Polls, Ltd., *Daily Mail* (London), July 13, 1964.

Foot (now Lord Caradon) has commented: "What a tragedy that Rhodesian leaders like Sir Roy Welensky failed when they had the chance to win the confidence of the Africans. What blindness that they made no serious attempt to do so—that they scarcely met the African leaders . . . In Southern Rhodesia until very recently there was a chance of cooperation between white and black. Blindness and obstinacy in Salisbury and lack of political courage in London threw away that chance. Now the drift has gone so far that it is difficult to see how it can be stopped short of violence." [9]

Questions for the United States

Rhodesia has an importance for American policy because of its bearing upon the direction, character and pace of political events throughout southern Africa. But America's direct economic and military interest is infinitesimal and its political and diplomatic influence not much greater.

The problem is essentially whether and to what extent to follow the lead of a close ally, Great Britain, in an area where it is influential and already deeply committed. In turn—assuming fundamentally compatible objectives between the United States and the United Kingdom in the situation—the problem becomes a matter of effective consultation and coordinated action. To date the United States has aligned itself fully with Britain, supporting its position in the United Nations and defending it against considerable criticism by the anticolonial majority. We have maintained that the situation in Rhodesia, although deteriorating, does not constitute a threat to international peace and security as the term is used in the U.N. Charter, and we have expressed confidence that Britain will be able to work out an acceptable solution.

The United States' position has been set forth by Paul F. Geren, former U.S. Consul General in Salisbury, in these terms:

First we recognize that Great Britain has a special concern and a unique influence in Southern Rhodesia. Second, we hope for continued political development along nonracial lines and the elimination of racial discrimination, so that each man may be judged on his merits

[9] *Saturday Review,* July 25, 1964, p. 11.

as a human personality. . . . Third, we hope there will be progressive development toward the eventual goal of universal adult franchise. . . . We acknowledge that the people of this country must determine the rate of advance toward that goal, but we hope that leadership from all sections of the community may participate in such determination of the rate. We concur with what has been said on so many sides: No new arrangement is likely to succeed without the support of African opinion. . . . Fourth, we hope Southern Rhodesia will have peaceful and mutually beneficial relations with its neighbors.[10]

The statement is unexceptionable, but it hardly conveys the sense of urgency now needed. In the past the United States has perhaps taken too dutiful and passive a stance in its dealings with Great Britain on the Rhodesian question. And if British policy should now return to a limp and permissive attitude, then the only sensible course for the United States would be to separate itself from its ally and seek an independent line of action. But so long as the new British government shows a serious inclination to act, the need is for vigorous American collaboration.

In the short run, a series of sharp-edged questions may arise. In view of the possibility of Rhodesia's imminent unilateral declaration of independence, are there new actions which the United States and Great Britain should take in an eleventh-hour effort to stave off disaster? Such initiatives might underscore in the plainest terms the penalties which Rhodesia will suffer by such illegal action as well as offer assistance and cooperation should its government begin to pursue programs in the spirit of racial reconcilation and eventual majority rule.

If nonetheless a unilateral declaration should come, how far should the United States go? The more drastic possibilities would include breaking all relations; imposing full economic sanctions, in company with Britain and other nations; and offering support to a representative Rhodesian group in exile. Or should the United States take a strong initiative in the United Nations to organize international pressure for the release of political detainees and for the removal of denials of political and other rights for the non-white Rhodesians? These are suggestive of the kinds of short-term problems on which, hopefully, the State Department and Whitehall

[10] Reported in *Africa Digest,* April 1964, p. 130.

are already in close and continuous consultation and joint planning.

If a detonation of the situation can be avoided in the near term, there must be longer-range efforts toward achieving a stable, legitimate, multiracial government in Rhodesia. The best prospect for the United States, both to use its limited influence in the Rhodesian situation and to protect its own interests from a damaging blow as a result of further deterioration, lies in strong British initiative to bring about, by negotiation if possible, constitutional reform and political change.

In 1964 a noteworthy series of essays was published by nine Rhodesians, both African and white, under the title *Southern Rhodesia —The Price of Freedom*. The editor in his preface wrote that the book "speaks in behalf of a section of the community who believes: (a) that it is not too late to achieve a peaceful transition toward a new order in Southern Rhodesia; (b) that it must be by negotiated agreement between representatives of different parties and races; (c) that no settlement is possible unless Europeans are prepared to name a date—a not too distant date—for majority rule, and unless Africans are prepared to accept and cooperate in a period of transition." [11] That statement of beliefs might well form the underlying premises of a longer-term American policy toward Rhodesia.

In full consultation with Great Britain and with neighboring states such as Zambia, the United States might take certain additional and complementary steps. It should make every effort to maintain and broaden channels of communication with the various elements of the African nationalist movement as well as with all segments of the white population of Rhodesia. It should widen opportunities for the education of Rhodesian African students abroad, and it should join with Great Britain in expanding training opportunities for Africans within Rhodesia itself. It should offer to serve as a third party "to help the various groups in Southern Rhodesia allay the deepening fears and mistrust. . . ." [12] Having made clear to the Smith government the consequences in terms of American reactions to a continued blind pursuit of its present course, the

[11] *Southern Rhodesia—The Price of Freedom* (Que Que, Rhodesia: Midrho Press, Ltd., 1964).

[12] Speech by Jonathan Bingham, reported in *United Nations Review*, October 26, 1962.

United States should clearly and consistently cleave to a base line of firmness on behalf of majority self-rule in all its dealings with that government. As a practical matter, general pressure and encouragement in behalf of movement toward political dialogue among the several elements of the Rhodesian population, and between them and Britain, is as far as U.S. policy should seek to go in involving itself in Rhodesian affairs. If and when concrete steps and agreed solutions arise from that dialogue, the United States should be prepared to assist in giving them effect.

Rhodesia represents a particularly tragic aspect of the fundamental problem of southern Africa, the inability and unwillingness of privileged minorities to relinquish their power and accommodate themselves to the forces of history. As Frank Clements, a former Mayor of Salisbury, said: "The European is not opposed to African social and economic advancement. . . . He has not, however, been able to accept the African's contention that advancement is inexorably linked with the exercise of political power."

In the breakdown of human relationships and communication the familiar pattern of polarizing attitudes has become manifest. Moderates have tended to disappear and middle ground to vanish. At the same time there is an instinctive if unexpressed awareness that the longer the white minority continues to cling desperately to power, the more certain that the final and inevitable transfer of political control will take place violently and will put government in the hands of an African majority inadequately prepared for its exercise. If there is still the possibility of building upon what remains of a tradition of racial cooperation and trust in Rhodesia a new workable and representative constitutional structure, then it will only be through the intelligent and powerful exercise of British authority and responsibility.

If it turns out that Rhodesia cannot be put on a constructive path to racial reconciliation, then the best test case for political evolution in southern Africa will have failed. The Portuguese colonies present problems that are far less amenable to influence by helpful external forces, and those of the Republic of South Africa are the most difficult of all.

Chapter IV

South Africa

At the southernmost tip of Africa lies a beautiful country, richly endowed in climate and resources, and currently enjoying a robust economic boom. But beneath the beauty and the boom lies a problem of human relations, ugly in its present reality and uglier still in its violent and destructive potentiality. Of all the problems congested in southern Africa this is by all measures the most complex, the most baffling, and the most far-reaching in its implications.

The Republic of South Africa is about twice the size of Texas and has a population of some 16 million, of whom about 12 million are Africans (in South Africa called Bantu), more than 3 million are whites, and the remainder are coloreds (mixed blood) and Asians (mostly Indians). The Africans are divided into three major tribal groups, the Xhosa, Zulu and Sotho. Of the whites, approximately 60 per cent speak primarily Afrikaans and 40 per cent primarily English.

The Afrikaner came to South Africa in the mid-seventeenth century from The Netherlands with the Dutch East India Company, which required provisioning facilities for its ships at the halfway point between Europe and the Orient. In three centuries he has become so much a part of Africa that he has long ceased to regard himself as a settler. During the seventeenth and eighteenth centuries, the Afrikaners were involved in a long series of skirmishes and battles against Hottentots, Bushmen, and later powerful Bantu tribes as they pushed inland to settle the country. After the Napoleonic wars, English settlers occupied the Cape. The subsequent struggle of Afrikaners against the newcomers and political control by Whitehall continued through the nineteenth century and culminated in the Boer War of 1899–1902, following which the Afrikaners accepted an uneasy partnership with the British in the new Union of South Africa. Finally, after World War II, the Afrikaners, through their National Party, took political control of the country. They have made the racial doctrine of apartheid the central feature of their domestic policy. This is the issue which led South Africa to withdraw from the British Commonwealth in 1961, so heavy was the criticism of other members, especially those with colored populations.

In the course of their long and bitter fight against the British the Afrikaners developed an intense and highly organized group solidarity. At the same time, cut off from world currents of political and social ideas, they acquired deep-seated and distinctive racial attitudes reflecting the relationships in the rural areas between the pioneering whites and primitive tribal blacks. The present Afrikaner political program has thus been born out of the sustained struggle and experience of a strong and proud people. The government they now control represents the most extreme, fierce and radically egocentric nationalism on the entire African continent.

The meaning of the doctrine of apartheid, which has become a matter of passionate international controversy, is seemingly simple but in fact exceedingly complex. The term itself means apartness or separateness in the development of the major racial groups. At a time when the idea of multiracial society based on equality is gaining worldwide acceptance the South African government is driving in precisely the opposite direction.

According to official statements the doctrine acknowledges the permanent position of non-whites in the South African complex and their right to progress. In the past, South Africa has probably done more than any other African country for secondary and higher education of Africans, not necessarily because of benevolence but because of the compelling need of the economy for trained personnel. It is envisaged that over the long term the political, social and economic aspirations of the African peoples would be met by constituting a system of separate Bantu homelands, or "Bantustans," within which they would enjoy a measure of self-government and administer most of their own affairs. To develop these separate areas the government has invested modest but increasing amounts for housing, irrigation, soil and water conservation, and agricultural development. The first of the Bantu territories—the Transkei —has already been proclaimed, and a legislature has been formed on the basis of a minority of elected members and a majority of chiefs who have official South African sanction.

While Africans will continue to live and work within the white areas of the country, there they have only a "temporary" status and no political rights. Their residence, employment and movement are subjected to an extensive system of regulations and restrictions.

The justification for apartheid as presented for foreign consumption rests on several historical, theoretical and practical grounds. First, the present dominance of whites is said to be justified by the fact that they have earned their position through their own labor and contribution to the development of South Africa. The land was poor and much of it unoccupied when they came to it, and they have established their own distinctive nationhood in a homeland which they have not taken from anyone.

Second, it is argued that cultural differences between the whites and non-whites are so great that it would be improper as well as impractical to intermix the contrasting elements or to absorb the one into the other. Thus it is claimed that apartheid does not deny the dignity and individuality of man but holds that each person should find these in the society he understands, namely his own racial group.

Third, it is said that apartheid, by offering the African separate rights and development, is an alternative to and an escape from white domination in a multiracial situation. It is therefore, according to this view, not born out of racial hatred and is the very reverse of the idea of white supremacy.

Fourth, apartheid is said not to be repressive of the African's economic and social aspirations because it provides him with increasing opportunity and training for skilled positions and professional work.

Fifth, although apartheid accords the African political rights only in the native reserve areas, it is asserted that these eventually can become full political rights since apartheid envisages a federation of viable Bantustans eventually joined with white South Africa in peaceful and equal association.

As to the sincerity and motivation of the policy, critics have pointed out a jarring discordance between the terms in which apartheid is defended abroad and those in which it is described at home. Thus, Prime Minister Verwoerd, speaking to the House of Assembly at Cape Town on January 25, 1963, stated: "Reduced to its simplest form the problem is nothing else than this: we want to keep South Africa white . . . 'keeping it white' can only mean one thing, namely, white domination—not 'leadership,' not 'guidance,' but 'control,' 'supremacy.' " [1]

Opposition to apartheid, which is considerable within South Africa and widespread throughout the world, denies every official justification for the policy on moral, philosophical, and practical grounds. Religious leaders of various faiths, including many in South Africa itself, have denounced it. It is condemned as a denial of the humane and democratic ideals which have characterized the Western world since the eighteenth century and which are now generally recognized in the U.N. Charter and the Universal Declaration of Human Rights. The doctrine is considered particularly pernicious at a time in history when people of varied races in many countries are attempting to work out patterns of interracial tolerance and cooperation.

The strongest arguments against apartheid are made on the factual grounds that it is impractical and unjust. Non-whites are already a majority in the cities of South Africa, and for demographic and economic reasons this proportion is destined to grow in the future, not decline. Thus, under the concepts of apartheid, the vast majority of Africans will be legally and permanently condemned to live as "temporary residents" without political, economic, or family rights in the white areas—which is to say four-fifths of the Republic.

Second, it is said to be unrealistic if not fraudulent to pretend that the Bantustans can ever accommodate the African population or provide them with economic or social opportunity. Although consisting of some of the country's better land, the Bantustans pres-

[1] Cited in *Report of Chairman, U.N. Special Committee on the Policies of Apartheid of the Government of the Republic of South Africa,* Document 64/07753.

ently constitute only 13 per cent of the territory of South Africa. Only about 40 per cent of the total African population now lives in the reserved areas, but overcrowding is already so great that nearly one-third of the families are landless. To expand the Bantustans to a scale where they could equitably accommodate the African population would be practically and politically impossible.

Third, the government's hope that the political aspirations of the African will be satisfied by the Bantustan concept is called pure wishful thinking. Perhaps the fatal weakness of the apartheid concept is that it makes no adequate provision for the political aspirations of the urbanized African who is the most educated, articulate, and politically minded element of the African population. Moreover, given the present mood throughout Africa, there is no reason to expect the non-whites of South Africa to be satisfied with an imposed, limited, and fundamentally controlled facsimile of independence, which is what the Bantustan concept offers.

On broader grounds and based on a mass of documentary evidence, it is charged that apartheid in practice is a system of brutal discrimination and exploitation. Under present South African laws the African has been effectively deprived of his fundamental political rights. He cannot vote in national or provincial elections; he cannot serve in Parliament; nor can he lawfully protest his deprivation or advocate political or social change even by picketing or other peaceful action. Similarly, his basic human and social rights are denied. His movement is strictly regulated by the pass laws, and his right to remain in any white area is subject to the most arbitrary administrative decision. He is limited to specified residential areas and to separate and commonly inferior schools, hospitals, and public accommodations. South African law makes it a criminal offense even for whites and non-whites to have tea together in a tearoom without a special permit. An African lawfully residing in a town by virtue of a permit must nevertheless obtain special permission to have his wife and children reside with him.

The African's economic rights likewise have been made meaningless. In most of South Africa he cannot acquire freehold title to land, and in the rural areas he is effectively reduced to serfdom by laws which make it a criminal offense for any African farm laborer to leave his employment without the written permission of his employer. In the cities he cannot as a worker bargain collectively, participate in a strike, or aspire to the higher and more remunerative positions. Over the African industrial worker hangs the permanent threat of governmental regulations which permit administrative officers at the stroke of a pen to determine that he is "politically suspect" and thereby take away his job and his livelihood.

Perhaps the most telling evidence against the contention that apartheid satisfies the African's aspirations is the fact that the governmental measures required to enforce apartheid against massive and growing discontent become more and more ruthless and degrading. South Africans, both black and white, accused of any of a number of loosely defined "political offenses" can be and frequently have been deprived of due process of law. The severity of some of the repressive measures which have been adopted is suggested by an evaluation of the General Laws Amendment Act of 1962 by the International Commission of Jurists. This bill, the Commission stated, "reduces the liberty of the citizen to a degree not surpassed by the most extreme dictatorships of the left or right. This measure is a culmination of a determined and ruthless attempt to enforce the doctrine of apartheid and is not worthy of a civilized jurisprudence."

Having heard the various contentions of the advocates and opponents of apartheid, world opinion has now passed unequivocal judgment upon it, condemning it both in its theory and its application. Today, even though diplomatic and economic relationships with South Africa are generally maintained, its moral isolation from the world community is nearly total. Never in modern times, and perhaps never in history—not even in the case of Hitler Germany or Stalinist Russia—has a government brought down upon itself so unanimously the moral disapproval of the world.

The closest thing South Africa has had to a strong and loyal friend over the years has been the British government. Yet Mr. Patrick Wall, a Conservative member of Parliament, speaking for the government at the United Nations in 1962, described apartheid as "morally abominable, intellectually grotesque, and spiritually indefensible." [2] And the next year the United Kingdom's Permanent Representative to the United Nations spoke of apartheid as "evil, totally impractical, and leading inevitably to disaster in South Africa itself. . . ." [3]

After fifteen years of charge and countercharge about apartheid, two facts at least are vividly and ominously evident: the world considers what South Africa is doing to its non-white people a violation of civilized principles; and, in the face of such sustained and general criticism, the South African government has not shifted from its course. Indeed, it appears to have become only more defiantly determined, and the situation is at an impasse.

The United States has come to a clear position on South Africa's race policy; in an address to the United Nations in October 1963, the late President Kennedy said: "We are opposed to apartheid and to all forms of human oppression." But no clarity has yet emerged as to what, if anything, the United States feels it should do about apartheid beyond asserting its general disapproval.

The United Nations and South Africa

Not surprisingly, the United Nations has been the forum in which the South African case has been argued before the world. The debate has pitilessly exposed both South Africa and the basic compromises and contradictions built into the Charter and the structure of the world organization.

By its nature the United Nations gives voice to both the powerful and the powerless states. Its Charter requires the member states to promote respect for human rights and fundamental freedoms; but it also assures them against intervention in matters which are essentially within their domestic jurisdiction. Basically directed to the settlement of international disputes by peaceful methods, it also provides for the use of "measures" against member states in certain circumstances, the precise definition of which is open to debate.

Step by step on the issue of South Africa, a majority of the mem-

[2] G.A.O.R., 4th Committee (1380th mtng.), A/C.4/S.R. 1380 (November 12, 1962).
[3] S.C.O.R. (1054th mtng.), S/PV. 1054 (August 6, 1963).

bers, led by the increasingly numerous African states, are testing the ultimate meaning of these provisions and the extent to which the United Nations can be used to force change upon a member state accused not of aggression but of unacceptable policy in the treatment of its own citizens. The first phase of their drive was to establish the right of the General Assembly to censure by general declarations the policy and practice of apartheid in South Africa. In the period from 1946 to 1960 such resolutions were passed by increasingly wide majorities and in ever stronger language. By the early 1950s the United States had conceded that racial discrimination in South Africa was an appropriate matter for U.N. consideration. And in 1960 after the Sharpeville shootings Britain, which had held fast to its position that apartheid was a matter within South Africa's domestic jurisdiction, shifted to join the majority in a resolution of censure.

The second step was to win General Assembly support for increasingly specific and forceful recommendatory resolutions. In 1960 the Assembly requested member states to consider taking such separate and collective action as is permitted under the Charter to bring about the abandonment of apartheid. In November 1962 the Assembly passed a resolution requesting member states to break diplomatic relations with South Africa, to close their ports and airports to its ships and aircraft, to boycott its goods and to prevent the export of arms. A year later the Assembly voted by a large majority to recommend that the member states apply an oil embargo on South Africa. Thus, by 1964 the African states had accomplished their second objective, namely, general approval of extensive voluntary sanctions against South Africa.

Parallel with their efforts in the General Assembly the African states have sought, through the Security Council, to win a third major objective, the imposition of *mandatory* sanctions against South Africa. They contend not only that apartheid is a violation of fundamental human rights which all members of the United Nations are pledged to respect, but also that the South African situation constitutes a "threat to the peace" within the meaning of Chapter VII of the Charter. Under this chapter the Security Council can require member states to take various economic measures against a transgressor, including interruption of economic relations and of communications, and the severance of diplomatic relations. No proposal has yet been put forward for the use of military measures against South Africa, which Chapter VII also permits.

In this effort, too, the African states have now made considerable progress. A most important step was taken on August 7, 1963, when by a 9 to 0 vote, with Britain and France abstaining, the Security Council decided that the South African situation was "disturbing to international peace and security" and called for an embargo on arms and ammunition. In voting for the resolution the United States made clear that it did so with the understanding that it envisaged action not under Chapter VII but under Chapter VI, which relates to the "pacific settlement of disputes" and with respect to which the powers of the Security Council are "recommendatory," not mandatory.

In December 1963 the Security Council requested the Secretary-General to set up a committee of experts to study methods of resolving the situation in South Africa by peaceful means. In April 1964 this group submitted its report which, among other things, recommended that the South African government be requested to convene a national convention representative of all its people to consider various remedial measures. It also recommended a study of the legal and practical possibilities of using economic sanctions to cause South Africa to change its racial policies. On June 19, 1964, the Security Council with the support of the United States and Britain voted to commission such a study, the two powers specifically stating that their willingness to see the study go forward represented in no sense an advance commitment to support coercive measures against South Africa.

As is often the case with U.N. statements, the final language of the resolution somewhat masks its considerable implications. Earlier resolutions called for members voluntarily to impose sanctions against South Africa, notably the embargo on oil shipments voted in December 1963. The resolution of June 1964, however, begins to lay a basis for possible compulsory action by the United Nations to force a member state to fulfill the Charter's human rights obligations. Despite the stated caveats of the American and British delegates, their affirmative votes represent a considerable shift of policy, particularly for the United Kingdom. Thus, although mandatory sanctions are still some distance and perhaps a great distance away, there is no doubt about the general direction of movement toward a broadened interpretation of the Charter and an extension of the range of issues on which mandatory measures may be considered.

If the trend continues much further, it can impose heavy strains on the United Nations; and if it does not continue further, the dangers to the organization may be equally serious. For the African states, joined by a large majority of others, the steps which have been taken over fifteen years represent a patient, reasonable effort to attempt by peaceful means and through U.N. machinery to do something about a situation in South Africa which they find intolerable. If a few of the major powers now block the possibility of going beyond general criticism and calls for voluntary action, the political atmosphere of the United Nations may become so inflamed that its essential comity could be destroyed. On the other hand, if the precedent is established that the United Nations can vote mandatory measures against any member state to compel it to fulfill the general principles and pledges of the Charter, then some of the major states may conclude that it has been transformed from an agency of carefully limited powers into an intolerable threat to their sovereignty, or at least an unjustifiable object of their financing and support.

The United States, as a major power with racial problems of its own and as a principal supporter of the United Nations, is consequently faced with momentous impending choices on the South African issue.

The Evolution of U.S. Policy toward South Africa

Until the 1950s South Africa was perhaps the one area of southern Africa with which the United States had some familiarity and direct relationship. As an ally in two world wars and as a member of the British Commonwealth, it was a country with which the U.S. government maintained direct and cordial diplomatic and military relations and with which American business had a limited but growing involvement. Since 1948, however, when political control of the country was won by the National Party, overwhelmingly composed of Afrikaners, relationships have become more complicated and strained.

Beginning in 1948, when the United States was in normal relationship with South Africa and considered that its racial problems were entirely its internal affair, American policy has moved a great distance toward the expression of open disapproval. As of late 1964, based on statements and votes in the United Nations and on other public declarations, the American position could be summarized as follows:

1. Apartheid is an offensive doctrine, contrary to a member state's obligations with respect to human rights under the U.N. Charter;

2. The South African situation is increasingly dangerous and could seriously trouble peace and progress in Africa and throughout the world if present trends continue;

3. The United States accepts the desirability of voluntary sanctions against South Africa in arms, machinery for their manufacture and strategic materials, and has itself largely cut off the sale of these items;

4. It is also prepared to have the Security Council study the possible feasibility of further sanctions against South Africa;

5. The United States makes financial contributions for the education of South African exiles and political refugees abroad.

In its direct relationships with South Africa the United States, however, continues in most respects to deal on a normal and "business as usual" basis. An embassy and consulates are maintained there; travel and educational and cultural exchange are encouraged by the United States; no barrier of law or executive policy exists with respect to trade or investment; and various forms of military and scientific cooperation are carried on.

In the continuing clash between South Africa and most of the rest of the world, the United States has frequently attempted to blunt criticism of South Africa and at the same time to exert persuasive influence upon the South African government to modify its position. On both counts American efforts have had minimal results. World criticism of South African policy has become more insistent and specific; and South Africa's position has only become more rigid and defiant. Judged by its results, the American policy of conciliation and mediation is at a dead end. The hard question is what to do next. It is time, therefore, to take a fresh look at the American interest in the South African problem, our policy objectives, and the measures whereby they can most realistically be advanced.

The Nature of American Interest in South Africa

Direct American economic and strategic interest in South Africa is far greater than in any other part of southern Africa; but it is still relatively small. American investment in the area totals some $415 million [4] or roughly 1 per cent of all U.S. foreign investment. Trade with South Africa currently amounts to about $500 million per year or a little less than $1\frac{1}{2}$ per cent of total U.S. trade. Military relationships are minimal since South Africa is not part of any American alliance and has no U.S. bases or forces on its soil. The agreements on scientific cooperation and strategic materials which continue between the two countries are of secondary importance.

Yet however slight its direct and material interests, the indirect and intangible interests of the United States are of substantial importance. For South Africa by its present policies has become the very symbol and quintessence of the race problem in the contemporary world. Apartheid is felt to be a direct affront to the dignity and self-respect of people of color everywhere, which is to say more than two-thirds of humanity. Further repression and bloody racial clashes in South Africa can inflame the feelings and harden the policies of all Africa and produce major political repercussions elsewhere. The obvious political and propaganda possibilities which this situation would create could be the door through which Communist influence enters the African continent in a decisive way.

Therefore, the South African problem is a world problem, not a local one; and its broad moral and political issues far outweigh, in terms of American national interest, the specifics of the situation itself. The intangible and the indirect aspects, not the material and the direct, constitute the core and substance of American national interest in the South African problem. What these considerations ordain must both in right and in reason guide American action.

The United States has consistently held that the ultimate solution must be worked out by the peoples of South Africa themselves on

[4] U.S. Department of Commerce, *Survey of Current Business,* August 1964. Figures are stated at book value.

the basis of a free and equal exchange of views among all segments of the population. This sensible objective is easy to state; but the difficulties in the way of its accomplishment are enormous.

Rightly or wrongly, the present controlling group in South Africa feels that to retreat from its commitment to apartheid, indeed to modify it in any fundamental respect, is to open the floodgates of catastrophe for the white population. Given the population statistics of South Africa and the course of development of the rest of the continent, they are convinced that any step toward sharing political power, even on some gradual or phased plan, will lead, probably sooner than later, to complete African control. In their view, any compromise will eventually bring about the destruction or evacuation of some three million whites.

To persuade them that evolutionary change does not necessarily mean the end of everything they and their forebears have built over three centuries is a task of extreme difficulty. It was not possible in the 1940s to persuade the Hindus and the Muslims of the Indian subcontinent to live together in the same state; there is little prospect that the Greek and Turkish groups in Cyprus in 1965 are about to settle their differences reasonably; and in the deep South of the United States the great powers of the federal government, the moral pressure of the bulk of the country, and the influence of sustained national prosperity have not had rapid effect in modifying the fundamental prejudices, fears and beliefs of the white population.

In South Africa racial attitudes have equally deep roots. Afrikaner defiance of the pressures of world opinion is not whimsical or merely mulish. On the contrary, in their view apartheid is the only conceivable policy for the country, given the basic demographic facts with which its white people must live. The English element has recently been moving to close ranks with the Afrikaners in defense of what they also are coming to consider a threat to their way of life. This reasoning rests on a deep substructure of emotions and fears, such as to make the racial problem seem almost insoluble by voluntary and rational processes.

In sum, the American interest in the South African problem is reasonably clear and substantial; and the policy objective to be hoped and worked for is well-defined. But the inherent intractability of the problem plus the necessarily limited influence an outside power can bring to bear on it eliminate any possibility of a quick or surgical solution.

The Prospective Calendar of Crisis

In the course of time the race problem in South Africa will be resolved either by constructive and evolutionary forces within the country or by violent and destructive ones, external as well as internal. Which are the more likely to prevail is difficult to say at present. But for American policy it is important to understand at least roughly the time scale of impending crisis.

Some liberal and optimistic South Africans see an encouraging number of constructive forces at work within the country. First and foremost, South Africa is still a democracy, as far as its white citizens are concerned. The judiciary has an honorable tradition of independence and integrity. The dominant National Party must cope with an organized and substantial political opposition for the support of the voters at national elections. The 40 per cent of the white population which is of English origin have not as a group historically shared the extreme racial views of the Afrikaners, although they are by no means united against these views. At the last general election in 1961 the National Party obtained some 370,000 popular votes; but the leading opposition party, the United Party, composed primarily of the English element, obtained 300,000 and the third largest party, which openly advocated the enfranchisement of all "qualified" citizens regardless of color, obtained 70,000 votes or nearly 10 per cent of the total. It is therefore argued that a change of only 10 per cent of the national vote in the next election, or a consolidation of the several splintered white opposition parties, would be sufficient to turn out the Verwoerd government and install a group committed to a race federation plan that would maintain Western standards and give non-whites an immediate participation and sense of function in government.

Another potentially important positive factor cited is the deeply religious feeling among the Afrikaner group and the power within the country of the Dutch Reformed churches. Some people believe that if internal repression should become much more brutal, church-led reaction against government policy might be significant.

Throughout South African society there are able and courageous liberal-minded individuals—men of affairs, intellectuals, women leaders, politicians, and others—who continue to exert themselves for constructive change. Too, a few South African newspapers have maintained a superb standard of reasonableness, responsibility, and independence in criticizing government measures and advocating changes in racial policy despite the serious risk of government reprisals.

At the deeper level of basic social and economic change other encouraging evidence can be cited. Among the Afrikaners the intense group solidarity of the past is being diluted by the forces of prosperity and modernism. Unlike the generation of the "Great Trek," they are increasingly urban, industrialized, middle-class people who in an ultimate showdown might conceivably choose, in Dr. Cornelis de Kiewiet's phrase, "the Volkswagen over the Volk."

As development and industrialization proceed, the economic interdependence of the races is increasing, not decreasing. The African population of South Africa is more skilled and enlightened than any in tropical Africa, and prosperous economic conditions will further assist their advancement. In the large urban areas non-whites already make up the majority of the population, and it can be shown that despite the intentions of apartheid, the mingling of whites and non-whites in the cities and in the economy will probably increase. So powerful is this tendency that, according to some leaders of the white community, the governing party dares not frustrate the process of growing interdependence among the races lest it undermine the basis of its white support and run the risk of checking or even reversing the favorable economic growth on which much of the strength of the South African position in the world now depends.

These are weighty contentions and considerations on the hopeful side. Yet the key question is not whether constructive forces exist but whether they are likely to prevail, and if so at what rate. In this regard, and on the less hopeful side, considerable evidence can also be adduced.

Prosperity has brought material benefits to Africans, lessened tensions to a degree, and increased economic interdependence; but it has also encouraged the present government in its adamant stand and has incidentally provided massive resources for the physical repression of the non-white population.

With respect to those able and determined South Africans opposed to apartheid, it is one thing to recognize and take encouragement from their existence; but the regrettable fact is that at present they seem to be on the defensive if not in retreat. They are subject to increasingly severe repressive measures, and the major opposition forces have shown a marked tendency in recent months to accommodate themselves more and more to the racial attitudes of the Verwoerd government. A growing fear of the future has brought the white community together more solidly in support of a white supremacy policy than ever before. Moreover, in assessing negative factors in the situation, the historical trend in South Africa is clearly in the direction of greater, not less, discrimination against the non-whites. Occasions have been presented repeatedly when the liberal forces of the country might have moved it to a new course in its race relations; but on such occasions they have consistently been overcome, a development parallel to other cases of recent history in which societies have become caught in the grip of a virulent and negative ideology.

Finally there is the question whether constructive internal forces, however strong they may be, can become operative and effective quickly enough to offset the continuing likelihood of violence and the intrusion of external factors which will tend to polarize attitudes and undermine moderating influences. It is earnestly to be hoped that constructive elements within the country will somehow succeed in saving South Africa from catastrophe. The definite prospect must be recognized, however, that these forces will continue to be overwhelmed and that in any event to re-establish communication among the various racial groups and to find some exit from the present dangerous impasse will take a considerable period of time. It would therefore be highly dangerous to base American policy on the cheerful assumption that liberalizing forces within South Africa will shortly take command.

Is it inevitable then, as some contend, that in the near future a massive explosion of race violence will occur, which in turn will result in revolutionary political change? Underlying such an expectation is the reasoning that the great majority of the population, which is made up of non-whites, has now been left by the Verwoerd government with no outlet for discontent other than violence. Every peaceful alternative has been closed off, and the brutality of the measures of repression has reached the point where they are intolerable. A recent sample survey of 150 middle-class Africans conducted by the South African Institute of Race Relations found that most of them are now prepared to accept violence as a method of political action, and nearly half believe that the use of force has become inevitable.

In the past three years incidents of planned sabotage and sporadic violence have become more frequent. Two underground organizations have been formed (with white leadership) which specialize in sabotage and hit-and-run attacks against industrial installations and communications. A third organization which claims a large African membership has concentrated on plans for mass rioting, including attacks designed to destroy property and to terrify whites. So far there is no cooperation among these groups, and because of differences over tactics and political orientation some friction has already developed among them.

South Africa, as it becomes increasingly industrialized and economically developed, necessarily becomes more vulnerable to sabotage. Re-enforcing the belief that sabotage may soon become a widespread danger is the fact that substantial and growing numbers of South African blacks are now being trained in these techniques in both the Soviet Union and in China and that they will shortly be returning to South Africa. The danger of immediate and large-scale violence has been strongly emphasized by high-ranking members of the Verwoerd government in urging increased appropriations for internal security purposes.

Despite this substantial evidence there is reason to view with some skepticism the probability that sabotage and violence within the next three to five years can bring the situation to full crisis or revolutionary solution. The government now has a complete system of legal measures to break the spirit and leadership of any opposition movement, to deprive it of access to the mass media, to confine or if necessary put to death its leaders, and to impose penalties of many kinds and of varying severity upon any participant in any protest action.

The recent history of totalitarian states gives convincing proof of the capacity of modern police methods to suppress dissident internal elements when applied ruthlessly and consistently. The South African police is well organized, armed with the most modern equipment, highly disciplined, and thoroughly versed in antisabotage and riot-control techniques. It is a highly mobile force with an authorized strength of 30,000 men, supported by a reserve understood to number 6,000 men. It has a sizable political branch which is empowered to open mail, tap telephones and search houses at any time, and an effective network of informers.

For purposes of controlling internal political disorder, the police and the armed forces can be considered as one. Total government expenditures for defense and police have risen from $112 million in 1960–61 to $294 million in 1963–64. This represents 26.8 per cent of South Africa's annual budget. In March 1964, Parliament was asked for the equivalent of $362 million for internal security and defense expenditures in 1964–65.

Perhaps more indicative of the political and psychological mood of the country than the capacity of its army and police to deal with physical disorder is the fact that among some three million whites there are now more than two million privately owned firearms. Special schools exist throughout the country where whites can learn methods of self-defense and the use of arms; and women's pistol clubs are reported to be in vogue. In its budgetary presentation of 1964 the government stressed its intention to train every white youth from the age of seventeen to fight. Thousands of others will be organized as "Kommandos" who will have rifles and emergency rations in their homes and farms so they can take up arms at a moment's notice.

Against such a bristling fortress of white preparedness the successful conduct of widespread sabotage would require quantities of equipment and trained saboteurs, highly developed organization and communications, and above all a passionate readiness on the part of non-whites not only to use violence but to sacrifice themselves if necessary to achieve their political objectives.

In this regard it is important to take into account the long tradi-

tion of forbearance and nonviolence on the part of the African
nationalist movements in South Africa. There has been an enduring reluctance among African leaders to embark on a program
of violence, to the point where many observers feel that they
have injured the Africans' cause by persisting in tactics of passive-
ness and persuasion long after there was any objective basis for
believing such methods would be effective. For the first forty years
of its existence the African National Congress confined itself entirely to constitutional methods of opposition. Only in 1952 did it
decide to join a campaign of passive resistance. In 1959 a group of
younger ANC members, formed a parallel organization, the Pan-
Africanist Congress, which was less committed to the nonviolent
approach. But both the ANC and PAC have since been banned
and are now obliged to work underground or in exile.

Undoubtedly the African devotion to nonviolence is passing if
not past. Even Chief Albert Luthuli, the Nobel Peace Prize win-
ner and a long-time advocate of nonviolence, said after the sen-
tencing of a number of African Nationalist leaders to life imprisonment in 1964, ". . . in the face of the uncompromising white refusal to abandon a policy which denies the African and other oppressed South Africans their rightful heritage—freedom—no one can
blame brave, just men for seeking justice by the use of violent
methods; nor could they be blamed if they tried to create an organized force in order to ultimately establish peace and racial
harmony." Thus, black leaders are at least in a mood to accept the
necessity of violence and are taking organizational steps in that
direction; but they are confronted by the almost overwhelming
power of the internal security system. Measures such as economic
boycotts and widespread strikes are conceivable in the near future.
But the kind of sustained, large-scale and desperate action by
the blacks which would be necessary seriously to threaten the physical control of the government would appear to require not months
but years to organize.

The availability of external assistance to revolutionary movements within South Africa can, of course, greatly affect the rate
at which they might develop. But this possibility too must be put
in some perspective of scale and time. The proposal repeatedly put
forth by one African state for a combined African military force

which could "invade" southern Africa has never been taken seriously by most African leaders. The enormous logistical problems confronting any direct military effort against South Africa, combined with the extremely limited military capacity of the independent African states at present, makes such an idea totally unrealistic. The Organization of African Unity, however, has undertaken to assist sabotage activity through the training of personnel and the provision of material. The scale of such help is not yet significant, but it might grow substantially over the next three or four years.

Both the Soviet Union and China have manifested intense interest in the South African situation. China, in particular, has offered substantial help of all kinds to saboteurs and guerrilla fighters. It is possible that the scale of such help could soon reach major proportions. However, the capacity of South Africa to intercept saboteurs, to tighten internal security controls, and if necessary to control radically the movement of all non-whites through measures ranging from curfews to regroupment camps, must not be underestimated.

For American policy, therefore, it is important to recognize the strong thrust now under way toward increasing violence in South Africa, and the mounting danger that such violence may produce widespread repercussions throughout Africa and in other parts of the world. However, the danger of "massive bloodshed and revolt," if it indeed becomes real, will probably not arise for a number of years—five to ten at a minimum and possibly twenty or more.

Hence, the South African problem is not likely to be solved—rationally or violently—for a long time. It is more likely to remain a festering sore for years to come, spreading its infection ever more widely and with ever greater danger to the peaceful functioning of the world community. And, the longer the problem goes unsolved, the more positions within South Africa will harden and the more difficult any solution will become. Thus, it would seem wisest for the United States to confront the problem now, in its present form, and take whatever prompt and feasible measures are available to influence the situation. Among such measures, first consideration must be given to the possible utility of economic sanctions.

Sanctions and South Africa

The current efforts of the Afro-Asian states in the United Nations focus on mandatory economic sanctions, which they appear to believe can exert sufficient pressure on South Africa to force a change in its policy of apartheid. They consider it politically feasible to organize and enforce such sanctions, which they argue would be justified on the ground that the situation in South Africa constitutes a "threat to the peace" within the meaning of Chapter VII of the Charter.[5] Each of these judgments or assumptions deserves the most careful scrutiny.

First, with respect to the probable impact on South Africa of international economic sanctions, there is little basis to believe that they can be of decisive importance, and even less that they will necessarily lead to constructive political change. The resiliency and adaptability of modern states to resist external economic pressures is considerable. In the case of both Japan and Germany in the late 1930s and early 1940s, there was a general tendency to exaggerate their vulnerability to such measures. The fact was that during World War II, despite the hammering of heavy aerial bombardment in addition to blockade, both countries managed to conduct a major war effort and to maintain their economic effectiveness for a long period of time. Since then the techniques of national economic mobilization, drawing upon wartime and subsequent experience in both mixed market and planned economies, have been further developed. Any economy in which internal order is reasonably well maintained has several lines of economic self-defense against external pressure, including the better utilization of underemployed resources, materials substitution, control of consumption, stockpiling, the postponement of retirement or renewal of capital equipment, and other measures. In addition, totalitarian countries can select "expendable" economic or social groups to cushion the remainder of the economy and society against shortages; in South Africa this point obviously has special relevance.

[5] The following pages discuss the possible application of sanctions against South Africa because of its domestic racial policies. The applicability of sanctions in relation to the South West Africa case is considered in Chapter VI.

The imposition of sanctions on South Africa or any country not involved in major hostilities faces the fundamental difficulty that such sanctions have to operate against the entire capacity of a mobilized economy whose only problem is to sustain its population at whatever subsistence level is required to maintain morale and public order. The South African economy is exceptionally well insulated against external economic compulsion. At present it is thriving and has great intrinsic strength with a strong agricultural and mineral base and an increasingly diversified industrial sector. The country is self-sufficient in its most essential foodstuffs and has the benefit of a vigorous and highly qualified supply of managerial and technical manpower.

The dynamo of the economy has been, and still is, gold mining. At present about 70 per cent of all the new gold produced in the free world comes from South Africa. This commodity by its physical nature is virtually impossible to boycott. As South Africa's most important export, it presently earns about $1 billion a year in foreign exchange which, in the event of sanctions, would provide the country with a powerful protective buffer.

If one of the purposes of sanctions is to injure South Africa's military capacity, then it is already two or three years too late for such measures to be crippling. Except to deal with major fighting for a protracted period, South Africa already appears to have all the armament which could conceivably be required for internal security purposes. In the past two years the government has begun a program of stockpiling matériel and has made substantial progress in developing domestic arms production.

The lack of petroleum reserves is often considered to be South Africa's principal economic vulnerability. But here again the country is protected to a considerable degree from the effects of an interruption of oil imports. At present 85 per cent of its economy is fueled by low-cost domestic coal, production of which could readily be increased. The government's industrial development corporation has created a company for the production of oil from coal which now produces some 8 per cent of the country's gasoline requirements. Under present development plans this output will double in the coming few years. Such fuel, although more expensive than imported petroleum, could ease the impact of an interruption of foreign supplies. In addition, an essential fraction of South Africa's oil requirements can now be obtained from recently developed oil production in Angola. By stockpiling oil, by stimulating the production of synthetic fuels, and by the further utilization of its coal resources—even if it should be unable to obtain adequate supplies of bootleg petroleum from abroad—the South African economy can probably withstand for an indefinite period even the effect of an oil embargo.

One of the factors in the rapid economic development of South Africa in recent years has been the availability of foreign capital. Cutting off this flow could have some impact, but the influx of capital to a country like South Africa, given the diversified and highly flexible international finance market, is technically and practically extremely difficult to control. Moreover, at present some 90 per cent of the country's capital requirements are estimated to be generated internally.

Thus, purely with respect to their economic impact, sanctions against South Africa can probably impose some inconvenience upon its economy, slow down its rate of economic growth, increase its costs, and force the government to adopt a general program of economic mobilization to divert consumption and production into priority areas. In addition, as a sharp indicator of world concern, they might produce psychological effects upon South Africans and their government. But there is no practical possibility, even if a comprehensive system of sanctions could be organized and applied, of striking a decisive blow at the country or of "bringing it to its knees," as some proponents have suggested.

Far more difficult than the economic aspects are the practical political problems of organizing and enforcing a system of international sanctions. Let it be assumed that in the United Nations there will be little difficulty in persuading the Afro-Asian states, all of which have relatively small trade with South Africa, to join in a program of mandatory sanctions. Assume, also—although the assumption is dubious, given the Soviet Union's attitude on previous issues involving the powers of the Security Council—that the legal advisors of the U.S.S.R. will have sufficient ingenuity to find a way to enable it to vote for mandatory sanctions. The key problem would still be the attitude of the major trading partners of

South Africa, which include some of the principal Western powers plus Japan.

For most of these countries the use of economic measures in behalf of political and foreign policy objectives is contrary to strong traditions and encounters heavy practical difficulties. The United States, probably more than any of the others, has tended to favor the use of economic instruments to deal with international problems and has on occasion taken strong leadership among its allies to that end. The results have been consistently unimpressive. Western economic restrictions against the Soviet Union and the Soviet bloc were never entirely effective and have now largely broken down. Similar restrictions against China have been resisted by many of the Western industrial countries despite strong American pressure. Still more recently, American efforts to organize and impose sanctions on Cuba have been openly defied by some of its closest allies, including the United Kingdom, France, and Spain. Nor have recent votes in the United Nations involving sanctions given evidence that these long-held attitudes of the Western countries toward collective economic measures have undergone change. If the proponents of mandatory sanctions are to avoid a great deal of wasted effort and energy, those plain and hard facts must be realistically assessed.

Finally, the advocates of mandatory sanctions assume that their effects in South Africa will be constructive and conducive to useful political change. There is regrettably little in the history of similar attempts to justify this optimistic expectation. In fact, the most probable effect of sanctions is simply to unify resistance in the state under siege. As Haile Selassie bitterly said to the League of Nations in 1936, the major consequence of the adoption of sanctions was to cause Italy to use poison gas to hasten its conquest of Ethiopia.

In their concern and frustration about the South African situation it is understandable that the Afro-Asians and all opponents of apartheid have sought to find some means short of military action to compel change in South Africa. General censure and voluntary sanctions adopted to date undoubtedly have been of some value in calling world attention to the situation in South Africa and in forcing morally sensitive nations like Britain and the United

States toward open disapproval of apartheid. But the present drive for mandatory sanctions through the United Nations raises serious doubt about the wisdom of the Afro-Asian course, even from the point of view of African self-interest. It is extremely un-likely that Security Council approval for mandatory sanctions on South Africa because of apartheid will be gained. Pressing the mat-ter excessively therefore may well accomplish less than nothing by giving South Africa an apparent victory in the United Nations, pro-ducing negative effects on the internal South African situation, or endangering the United Nations itself.

Sanctions and U.S. Policy

The United States has already crossed the bridge of voluntary sanctions, and further desirable actions of this character will be suggested later. But in the United Nations, taking account of the current Security Council study of sanctions completed in 1965, a clear policy decision with respect to mandatory sanctions against South Africa may have to be faced on the grounds that the policy of apartheid constitutes a "threat to the peace."

The United States has already declared that the situation in South Africa, "though charged with somber and dangerous impli-cations, does not today provide a basis under the Charter" for such sanctions. Further, the United States has made clear that it cannot "support the concept of an ultimatum to the South African govern-ment which could be interpreted as threatening the application of coercive measures in the situation now prevailing, since in our view the Charter clearly does not empower the Security Council to apply coercive measures in such a situation." [6]

It is vital that, unless the South African situation should radically change, the United States continue to hold fast to that difficult but responsible position. The grounds for this conclusion are three, in addition to the factual probability that such sanctions would worsen, not improve, the present situation and might provoke bloodshed without useful result.

First, such sanctions, if they are effectively enforced, inherently

6 Statement by Ambassador Adlai E. Stevenson before the Security Council, June 16, 1964 (U.S./U.N. press release 4415 and corr. 1).

contain the danger of further measures of compulsion and the eventual use of military force. To adopt mandatory sanctions in the cynical expectation that they would not be enforced would be a reckless and irresponsible use of the ultimate powers of the United Nations as an instrument of collective security. On the other hand, effective enforcement—by the special nature of the South African case—would in all probability ultimately mean blockade. In addition to the heavy cost of patrolling more than 2,000 miles of distant South African seacoast, highly inflammatory incidents would inevitably occur, given South Africa's naval and aircraft capacity. As Mr. William Gutteridge has written, "A blockade itself might be the signal for a rising or inability to export might lead to mass African unemployment and consequent civil unrest. The result would be bloodshed, perhaps full-scale civil war arising from U.N. action. The responsibility to restore peace would be clear and, with desperation on both sides of the racial fence, this would involve massive intervention on a scale far greater than that in the Congo. It would not be possible to rely entirely on the neutralist states; the great powers would have to bear the brunt. . . ." [7]

Military conflict on this scale would eliminate whatever small possibility now exists for a constructive solution to the problem of race relationships in South Africa. No occupying military force, international or otherwise, could do more than preside over an appalling tragedy. Moreover, it is unjustifiable for the United States as a major and responsible world power to give its endorsement in a time of nuclear weapons and general international tension to any proposal so pregnant with major military dangers.

Second, to consider the racial policies of South Africa to be a "threat to the peace" justifying mandatory measures under the U.N. Charter is a proposition unacceptable on constitutional grounds. However morally offensive apartheid may be, it is not a direct and aggressive danger to other nations according to any standard familiar to law or diplomacy. South Africa by its racial policies is inflaming passions throughout the non-white areas of the world, and may be guilty of "incitement to aggression." But its conduct to date cannot be called a threat to the peace by any reasonable in-

[7] *Manchester Guardian Weekly,* July 2, 1964.

terpretation of the Charter. Indeed, if there is a threat to the peace in this sense caused by apartheid, it is largely a result of the attitudes of the independent African states, not of South Africa. Thus, constitutionality and the whole structure of concepts and intentions upon which the U.N. Charter has been built would be left a shambles by acceptance of the rationale which has been put forward.

Obstructive legalism has sometimes been a fault of the approach of some of the major Western powers to issues before the United Nations. But to contest the legitimacy of using the mandatory powers of the Security Council in the manner which has been proposed is no resort to technicalities. It goes to the bedrock basis of the United Nations at the present stage of history. If that basis is destroyed, then the present structure of collective security cannot stand.

Third, forcing a decision on mandatory sanctions by the Security Council would impose upon the United Nations pressure of an extremely severe kind at a time when the very survival of the organization is already challenged by a multiplicity of strains and crises. On occasion in the past, even in the face of major and *bona fide* threats to the peace, the United Nations his wisely turned away from the attempt to exercise its mandatory powers on the grounds that to do so would have destroyed the organization or would have increased, not lessened, the dangers to peace. Hungary, Cuba, and Tibet were such instances. And in the case of the U.A.R. or of Indonesia at the present, despite the avowed intention of those governments to destroy neighboring states and the vigorous development of military programs with that apparent purpose, the permanent members of the Security Council have felt it better to refrain from attempting to use the ultimate powers of the United Nations.

All the reasons and practical wisdom which have governed the conduct of the United Nations in such situations in the past obtain to an even greater degree in the case of South Africa, where open aggression against other states is not involved and where, on the contrary, extremely complex and fundamental constitutional questions must be raised. The Afro-Asian nations therefore must make a difficult and ultimate judgment: whether in their individual and collective interest they wish to risk damaging the United Nations in the effort to force change in South Africa; or whether to spare the United Nations that danger and seek to carry out their determination through other organizations and instrumentalities, such as the OAU.

For the United States to take a clear and steady stand against mandatory sanctions against South Africa will inevitably subject it to criticism and perhaps to some propaganda defeats. But any other course than rejection of such measures would be a violation of its own responsibilities as a world leader and contrary to the interest of its own citizens and of all mankind.

A Course for the United States

Mandatory sanctions against apartheid within South Africa represent an ultimate boundary across which the United States under present circumstances should not step. But short of that boundary lies a great variety of individual and collective measures of differing severity which the United States should urgently consider.

In a statement on June 12, 1964, after the Rivonia sabotage trials in South Africa, Chief Albert Luthuli concluded with the words: "In the name of justice, hope, of truth and of peace I appeal to South Africa's strongest allies, Britain and America. . . ." In part the phrasing of his appeal reflected an intelligent African nationalist strategy of thrusting the United States and Great Britain into the center of the stage on the South African issue, not only because of their important ties and influence, but because by the nature of their governments and social systems they are the most likely to be responsive to the moral aspects of the problem.

Nevertheless, in the minds of many people around the world, including the whites of South Africa, there is a considerable degree of verisimilitude if not of truth in Chief Luthuli's designation of the United States as one of his country's chief allies. For the fact is that although the United States has repeatedly expressed criticism of apartheid in recent years, it has simultaneously appeared to contradict its statements by other actions, with the result that it has now almost totally destroyed both its persuasiveness with the government of South Africa and the confidence of the African nationalists and the Afro-Asian states in the sincerity of its moral and political assertions.

The United States has been inconsistent in its stand on international human rights issues. In the late 1940s and early 1950s, it took strong initiative on such matters, but through most of the 1950s it shifted to almost total passivity. It has appeared to be a reluctant critic of racial injustice in South Africa; and, until pressed strongly in the United Nations, it took no action independently or through the organization to indicate its repugnance to apartheid. And even then, after criticizing South African racial policy, it has continued to deal with that government on a normal diplomatic basis, accommodating itself in many ways and with little protest to South African practices of discrimination. By its efforts to maintain a position of *interlocuteur valable* the United States has inadvertently but implicitly become an agent and spokesman in defense of South Africa in many international discussions and debates.

Therefore, if both the South Africans and the rest of the world are unconvinced even of the serious American desire to see change in the racial practices of South Africa, their skepticism is comprehensible. By its apparent halfheartedness the United States has indubitably tarnished its moral prestige in the eyes of much of the world. And if the intention has been to influence South Africa to change its policies by maintaining the posture of mediator and conciliator, then the results have been worse than fruitless. It has not produced a single alteration in the basic racial policy of the South African government, which has been far from appreciative of the American posture. As it increasingly feels itself under pressure, the Verwoerd government becomes increasingly paranoid; its denunciations in private and in public of American "treacherousness" become more acid and more frequent.

South Africa has come to be a complete liability to the United States and the West, and the United States should cease throwing its good name and moral prestige to the four winds by continuing its futile attempt to deal with that country on a "normal" basis. By a general clarification and coordination of its relationships with Africa the United States now must seek to re-establish and rebuild the credibility of its declared objectives and policy. This should be done not in the vain hope that it or any external factor can *force* change in South Africa by nonviolent methods; but rather in the clear recognition that America's self-interest requires the abandonment of the effort to carry water on both shoulders. Only by so doing can the United States hope to influence the South African government to alter its policies, or to have any moderating effect upon those of the black African states. More concretely, six lines of action are suggested.

First, by confidently taking the initiative the United States should begin to manifest its strong interest in human rights issues in all appropriate settings of the United Nations and elsewhere. Not one of the more than twenty-seven resolutions regarding South Africa's racial policies adopted by the United Nations since its inception has been initiated by the United States; and in all the organs of the United Nations concerned with problems of human rights the proposals initiated by the United States in recent years have been extremely few. This country has thereby been delinquent in upholding one of its most distinguishing characteristics and national interests. Is there any necessary reason why the United States cannot take the lead in advancing new proposals on human rights, with respect not only to South Africa but also to other problems around the world, many of which members of the Afro-Asian bloc for various reasons have been reluctant to bring forward? At a time when the United States has adopted new and advanced civil rights measures and is making a general attack on poverty and discrimination at home, there is no reason why it should not begin to lead from strength and raise, not lower, its voice on matters of human dignity and the rule of law throughout the world.

Second, the United States should cease being inactive and immobilized on South African matters except when driven or embarrassed into some action by pressures within the United Nations. If for good and sufficient reasons the United States believes that sanctions through the United Nations are an awkward or dangerous approach, then a multitude of opportunities remain for individual national action or cooperation with groupings other than the United Nations to exercise pressure upon South Africa. One possibility is for the United States to join with some of its Western

allies, including the Scandinavian countries, to devise such measures. Joint measures with France, Italy, Belgium and Switzerland
to extend the effectiveness of the arms embargo on South Africa
would be a concrete possibility. Such measures might be the more
useful and acceptable in South Africa by the very fact that they
would derive from a source other than the United Nations.

Cooperation between the United States and Great Britain is
particularly important. British trade and investment in South
Africa is several times as great as America's and Britain has
additional leverage as a result of long historical, cultural and family ties. At the same time, because of the magnitude of its economic
interests in South Africa and the strength of sympathy and sentiment in Britain for South Africans of English origin, Britain is in
a particularly difficult situation to take decisive action, a fact of
which the United States must be sensitively aware. Nevertheless,
there might be fruitful possibilities of collaboration between the
two countries on measures to reduce certain trade preferences now
accorded to South Africa or to tighten and make total the present
arms embargoes. In the past, through such actions as the famous
"wind of change" speech of Prime Minister Macmillan, Britain has
exerted powerful moral influence on South Africa, and in at least
one instance joint British and American effort has been productive
in causing South Africa to alter its tactical position on an important matter.[8]

Another promising possibility may be cooperation in initiatives
with some of the independent African states. There is evidence
that several of them are increasingly interested in individual
or collective action against South Africa outside the United Nations. U.S. cooperation with African states is now considerably
more difficult to organize following the Stanleyville incident of
late 1964, but all the more important for that reason to attempt.
Of the numerous possibilities some would be of small scope, such
as finding employment opportunities in Africa for South African
refugees now in Europe and the United States. Others would be of
greater impact, such as joining forces to advance the establishment

[8] This related to the application of the recommendations of the Odendaal
Commission. See Chapter VI, pp. 118–119, below.

of a United Nations presence in technical assistance in South West Africa.

Third, within the American government, initiative could be taken to identify and reassess the many measures of assistance now offered to South Africa including strategic materials contracts, scientific cooperation, and military cooperation. Steps might then be considered to cut off all those which do not make a clear net contribution to American national interests.

Fourth, in the complex field of economic relationships, a re-examination of present policies is required. As matters now stand the United States is in a thoroughly ambiguous position. For example, it supports a U.N. study of the feasibility of sanctions against South Africa, but it continues to accord to American investors every facility to transfer capital to South Africa. The United States, as part of its foreign policy, applies controls which restrict the commerce and investment of American citizens in a number of countries, but Washington has taken no measure thus far to interfere with, or even to indicate its particular disapproval of continuing American investment in South Africa.

In view of the state of official policy, some of the criticism which has been made of American private companies operating in South Africa is both unfair and indiscriminate. New investment by private American groups at the present time can justifiably raise questions not only about their business judgment, given the uncertain political future of South Africa, but also about their motives in placing capital in a situation of economic exploitation of the non-whites. But for many of the American companies now in South Africa it must in fairness be recognized that they made their investments in the period prior to the advent of the National government and the adoption of apartheid; and that their capital is often in the form of immovable property and assets which could be sold only at heavy losses to their stockholders. To call upon them to disinvest is therefore unrealistic. Even the problem of their reinvestment of profits cannot be considered without reference to the fact that in many cases such reinvestment is not entirely a matter of choice. Under South African exchange controls restricting the transfer of funds, reinvestment may be the only alternative to involuntary accumulation of doubtful government securities.

To clarify the situation there are several steps which the U.S. government might consider:

a) Cease immediately any further assistance or encouragement to new American investment in South Africa, including the extension of Export-Import Bank credits and other financing; and suspend all expenditure of government funds to promote trade and investment with South Africa.

b) Inform every potential American investor of the dangers of instability in the country, the inability of the U.S. government to protect American economic interests in the event of possible future disturbances, and the general disadvantages to the United States for American capital to move into such a troubled political situation. It is not impossible, for example, that American-owned factories in South Africa may be required by South African government order to participate in the manufacture of arms and equipment to be used in the suppression of the non-white population. Such a position could be injurious to the United States as well as to the companies themselves.

c) Urge every American company operating in South Africa to present a creditable example of wage, employee, and race relations policy. Granted that the companies must conform to local laws if they are to operate, within those limits they can set a better rather than a poorer example of American values and practices.

d) Urge every American investor or company to refrain insofar as possible from direct involvement in the administration of apartheid laws or policies through membership on quasi-official boards or commissions dealing with matters affecting wages or working conditions of non-white employees. Above all, American business representatives in South Africa should be officially urged to refrain scrupulously from political or other statements which can be exploited by the South African government.

These are minimal steps which might have to be followed by more specific legal prohibitions if the South African situation should further deteriorate. If the United States government by its sluggishness or passivity should fail to take even such limited measures, then it would be strongly in the interest of the American business community itself to urge such action.

The 1 per cent of American overseas investment now placed in South Africa is already beginning to affect adversely a substantially greater amount of American economic interest in Africa north of the Battleline and in other less developed areas as well.[9] Many of the companies investing in South Africa, including some of the major mining interests, themselves have investments elsewhere in independent Africa which may be jeopardized by their South African involvement. Other American companies, including several of the major petroleum producers which have important interests in independent Africa, are likely to find increasingly that American investment in South Africa is an embarrassment, and potentially a direct danger to those interests. Frail and limited in their economic resources, the African states have a continuing concern with encouraging foreign investment to assist their national economic development. Nevertheless, they are clearly moving in the direction of requiring every American and foreign company doing business there to make a clear choice between doing business in South Africa or enjoying concessions and trading privileges in other areas of the continent. The decision at the OAU meeting of July 1964 looking toward a program of secondary boycotts was a danger signal. American business as a whole, therefore, has a stake in pressing a more realistic and less contradictory South African policy upon Washington. Otherwise, it may unwittingly permit a tiny fraction of the American financial and business community to injure the interests and future opportunities of the vast majority.

The adoption of such restrictions and limited measures by the United States obviously will not impose meaningful economic penalties on South Africa. Its economy does not desperately need American investment, and if American investors should turn away, others from West Germany, France, Japan and elsewhere will probably be prepared to take their place. But they will have an importance in indicating that American disapproval of apartheid is genuine, coherent, and consistent. In this sense larger U.S. political and economic objectives will be served.

[9] Some comparative figures concerning U.S. investment in Africa and elsewhere are highly suggestive. Compared with $415 million in South Africa, U.S. direct investment in the rest of Africa totalled roughly $1 billion at the end of 1963, much of it in the Copperbelt and in North African oil. As late as 1950 there was an approximate balance between the two totals. U.S. investment in South Africa tripled between 1950 and 1963; in the rest of Africa it increased nearly sixfold. Since 1961, however, U.S. investment in South Africa has increased 33 per cent and in the rest of Africa 34 per cent. (U.S. Department of Commerce, *Survey of Current Business,* August 1964.)

As a fifth line of action the United States should consider shifting the present basis of its official educational and cultural exchange relationships with South Africa to the pattern of reciprocity successfully devised and used with the Soviet Union. As matters now stand, by dealing with South Africa on the same basis as Britain or France for example, U.S. policy implies that such exchanges are on a free and open basis. In fact, however, the South African government applies to the greatest feasible extent its racial and ideological doctrines to all such exchanges, including those financed by the United States government. It is made extremely difficult for non-whites and those out of sympathy with the present government to travel or study in the United States, while the admission to South Africa of Negroes or of other Americans who have expressed unfavorable views on apartheid is frequently blocked. If American private groups choose to continue their cultural and educational exchange programs with South Africa in order to help maintain some channel of communication with that country, they should not be discouraged. However, they should attempt to ensure that their efforts are not made subservient to the interests and the ideology of South Africa through its use of passport and visa controls.

Sixth, the United States should make far greater effort to develop direct contact and communication with opposition political groups and with African nationalist leaders both within the country and in exile in various parts of Africa and elsewhere.

The Communist movements of the world are making exceptionally heavy investments in developing such contact with the nationalist elements in South Africa. Viewed over the long term, it would be a major calamity if South Africa is finally taken over by its non-white majority under violent circumstances and the new leadership is connected with one or another of the elements of the world Communist movement. The industrial and economic capacity of a Communist-led South Africa would be quite sufficient to make that country immediately influential through large parts of Africa. As matters now stand, the Chinese and the Russians appear to be conducting a program of activity involving the nationalist leaders of South Africa about ten times as great as that of the United States. This implies the need for action on at least three fronts:

a) That the United States substantially step up its educational, cultural and exchange activities for black South Africans now in training or in exile outside of South Africa;

b) That the United States through private organizations of all kinds attempt to widen and maintain lines of contact and sympathetic communication with the African population in South Africa; and

c) That the United States, through its Voice of America and other official information efforts, strengthen its campaign to convey an undistorted picture of its policies to the majority of South African citizens.

American private groups with an interest in the South African situation—including church organizations, labor unions, and others—have many possibilities of initiative and useful action which have never been exploited. Even though such groups are not constrained by the same considerations as are American officials in speaking out on matters of racial injustice and human rights, they have too often remained silent.[9] They have thereby accentuated the impression in the world that the United States, despite its pretensions to world democratic leadership, tends to be indifferent to moral issues except where its direct national and strategic interests are involved.

Having taken these several difficult steps along the six lines of suggested action, what then will the United States usefully have accomplished in behalf of its own interests and toward resolving the problem of apartheid? Hopefully the results could be the following:

It will have made clearer to South Africa and to the world that the American nation seriously and genuinely disapproves of racialism and the violation of human rights within any society, Communist or non-Communist, white-controlled or black-controlled.

It will for the first time have brought the weight of its moral influence to bear on the white population of South Africa, making clear to the supporters of apartheid that South Africa can expect no cooperation from the United States so long as it follows its repugnant racial policy.

It will have demonstrated to the Afro-Asian states and others that the United States is sincerely opposed to racial injustice; and that,

[9] For an excellent listing of possible actions by private bodies see *The Future of South Africa, a Study by British Christians* (London: SCM Press, for the British Council of Churches, 1965).

on the other hand, as a responsible world power it will not give its endorsement to measures of force which can endanger the peace or jeopardize the existence of present institutions of collective security.

Finally, it will have brought American foreign policy on questions of racial justice into line with the sentiment and domestic policies of the United States itself. The United States would thereby have gone a considerable distance in recovering from the damage to its moral prestige which its ambivalent policies toward South Africa have to date inflicted upon it.

In sum, the United States by these actions would for the first time have begun to apply serious persuasive influence upon South Africa. Before rushing to more costly and dangerous measures to "do something" about the South African situation, or before denouncing such a moderate approach as futile, it would be only reasonable to try it. If in fact there are able, devoted and powerful liberal-minded white groups in South Africa eager to lead the country in a new direction in its racial policies, then perhaps the shock effect of such clear American disapproval of apartheid—especially if coordinated with measures from the United Kingdom and other Western countries—might produce positive results. If such political forces are weak or if their efforts are overwhelmed by the negative factors of violence and repression, then the United States will only have cut its present losses by a degree of disengagement from South Africa and have put itself in a better position to deal influentially with further phases of that problem as it unfolds. Seen in its international perspective, apartheid is both offensive to the world and inherently unjust; but it does not justify measures which would incur the danger of war to exterminate it. And, seen in the perspective of time, the likelihood of the effective application of measures short of force upon South Africa may be far greater after some of the other and relatively less difficult problems of southern Africa are resolved.

It may be objected that the course here recommended is too conservative and fatalistic. Or that it deals only with the extremes—rejection of military efforts and mandatory economic sanctions on the one hand and a contradictory and passive attitude on the other. Merely to achieve clarity on the need to reject such extremes would not be an inconsiderable improvement; but there are those who feel that the vital and relevant area to consider is the large and still obscure middle zone of possible action: partition of the country; acceleration and extension of the Bantustan concept; federative solutions involving the High Commission Territories as well as South Africa; and specific, negotiated modification of certain discriminatory legislation, including the pass laws, acts reserving skilled jobs for whites, and the Bantu Education Act.

It is possible, even likely, that the South African government may come forward with varied measures modifying present racial policies, especially if internal and external pressures increase in the future. The United States must be prepared to react to any such proposal on its merits. The United States should also stand ready to join with Britain or others to serve as external guarantors of adherence by all parties to any agreed political settlement within South Africa. But that is not to say that the United States should undertake to propose specific modifications of South African policy, or to enter into negotiations with the Verwoerd government to exchange American approval for mere ameliorations of apartheid.

Our general attitude in behalf of racial justice and government based on the consent and participation of the governed must be clear and consistent; and our influence, or pressure, should be steady and modulated in behalf of the opening of a political process and a search for solutions by the people of South Africa to their own problems.

In time, out of this course may come acceptable progress, or none. As political changes take place in other parts of southern Africa, including the High Commission Territories and South West Africa, new and significant opportunities may appear by which the United States can exert influence and induce constructive change. Or the situation may deteriorate, and in time drastic measures now regarded as unacceptable may have to be considered.

Thus the course recommended will be emotionally unsatisfying to many who feel impelled to urge acceptance of larger risks and to intervene more forcefully or specifically. For it is a course of limited measures, predicated on the need to weigh risks and costs as well as to pursue great objectives, aware both of the limitations of foreign policy as well as of human capacity to forecast the varied directions which development may take, and grounded in the faith that it is important both to be guided by clear ultimate objectives and to deal with concrete decisions on a practical basis.

Any course of policy, including the most moderate, involves risks which must be calculated. The steps recommended might well have to be carried out in an atmosphere of mounting frustration throughout the world about the injustice and repression in South Africa, and in the face of growing dangers of Communist penetration. But until such dangers become markedly more pronounced, the American view must be that this country must not hinder, though it cannot produce, necessary political change in South Africa. Such change, if it is to occur, must depend primarily upon constructive forces in South Africa, or on the heroism, sacrifice and, if necessary, bloodshed of the now oppressed majority of that country's citizens.

Although the world in recent decades has made progress in the recognition of universal human rights and in the development of interdependence and cooperation, it is still to a great extent a world of national sovereignties. Within the walls of its own sovereignty a country is still substantially able to determine its own course, particularly if it is strong enough to resist the external pressures which may be brought to bear against it. Some see in this fact a regrettable obstacle to man's well-being; others see in it his most precious safeguard of freedom and diversity. The policy course here recommended is therefore a rejection of the idea that some *deus ex machina* in the form of the United Nations or the United States or the United Kingdom can or should impose its will upon South Africa even for the noble objective of liberating the majority of its population from brutal oppression.

Chapter V

The High Commission Territories

Three fragments of land—remnants of Britain's African empire—may for the first time soon begin to play a role of some consequence in the political affairs of southern Africa. They are the protectorates, or High Commission Territories, of Basutoland, Bechuanaland and Swaziland, with a combined population of 1.3 million, overwhelmingly non-white. Their present significance derives from their geographical location within or bordering on the Republic of South Africa, as well as from the constitutional changes now occurring in them.

Basutoland, politically the most advanced of the three, is a small mountainous area about the size of Belgium, an enclave entirely surrounded by South Africa. Now moving rapidly toward independence, it has become a refuge for political fugitives from South Africa, whose authorities see it as the operational headquarters of underground organizations seeking to overthrow their government by violence.

Swaziland, another small territory surrounded by South Africa except for a seventy-mile border with Mozambique, is also moving forward in its constitutional development, but under the predominant influence of conservative African and white elements. If Basutoland opens the possibility of disruptive subversive influence within South Africa, Swaziland offers the opposite possibility of willing political collaboration with it.

Bechuanaland, an extensive and arid area on the northern flank of South Africa, is strategically the most important of the three territories. More than half as large as South Africa itself, it has roughly 1,000 miles of common frontier with South Africa, 500 miles with South West Africa, 500 miles with Rhodesia, and a vital few hundred yards with Zambia. It thus provides a direct link between South Africa, the heartland of apartheid, and the independent African areas to the north. It could become a corridor for the smuggling of arms, the escape of political refugees, and the passage of persons trained in agitation and sabotage.

As all three areas are intimately connected with South Africa, and economically dependent on it, they are highly vulnerable to pressures which it may exert. Basutoland, the poorest, exports its wool, mohair, and a few agricultural products mostly to South Africa. At any given time roughly two-thirds of its able-bodied men are at work in South Africa, and most of the cash income of the territory derives from their remittances. Swaziland, richer than Basutoland in the fertility of its soil and in mineral resources, exports two-thirds of its products to South Africa, and some ten thousand Swazi males work in South African mines and industries as migrant labor. The principal enterprises of the country are organized by its six thousand whites, many of whom are South African citizens and normally reside in the Republic. Bechuanaland sells most of its modest exports of beef, agricultural products, and minerals to South Africa and also depends upon it for the employment of some 20 per cent of its able-bodied workers.

The three territories have postal, rail, and other communication links with South Africa and depend on it for their electric power. They participate in a customs and currency union with the Republic, and together they receive a percentage of its customs collections constituting a considerable share of their revenue. Consequently, by measures clearly within its competence, South Africa could exert powerful, perhaps crushing economic pressures on the territories should it so choose. It could recalculate the customs and excise revenues now allocated to them, or alter the system of import quotas. Most important of all, it could establish new restrictions on the employment of migrant labor. Such a measure would, of course, impose economic costs on South Africa, which has a chronic and continuing shortage of labor for its booming economy. But under various conceivable political circumstances, these are costs which South Africa might be willing to accept.

Beyond economic measures, South Africa could impose other disadvantages upon the territories, ranging from intensified border restrictions and interruption of services and communications to political or even physical intervention. Thus, while the territories are capable of generating political irritations, perhaps even serious dangers, for South Africa, the latter could retaliate with measures of devastating impact upon them.

The Pattern of Political Change

The three protectorates came under British control in the latter half of the nineteenth century. In order to frustrate German and Boer ambitions in southern Africa, to regulate tribal disorders, or to protect the tribes at their request from incursions of white settlers in the neighboring areas, Britain successively—and somewhat reluctantly—accepted jurisdiction over them.

When the Union of South Africa was formed in 1909, it was assumed by Britain and specifically mentioned in the Act of Union that the three territories would ultimately, and with the approval of the inhabitants, be incorporated into the new state. For the following fifty years the territories lived, and London administered their affairs, in the general expectation that they were in transition to annexation by South Africa. As a result, Britain's treatment of them differed substantially from that of its other African colonies. Neither economic development nor political preparation was actively promoted. British officials interfered as little as possible with the customary powers of the native chiefs, whose position has remained unusually strong to the present day. Not until the 1930s did British public opinion begin to be concerned about conditions in the territories, and assistance to their economic development did not begin until the 1950s.

In recent years, however, the assumptions underlying British policy have been swept away. Growing repugnance in Great Britain for the racial policies of South Africa, combined with an intensification of the application of apartheid within the Republic, has made British consent to annexation impossible. Within the territories the clamor for economic and political change has become insistent, and in response Britain has been forced into a series of improvised steps to bring its policies into line with current realities.

Thus in 1960 Britain accorded Basutoland a new constitution and a considerable degree of autonomy; the following year it did the same for Bechuanaland. And in 1963 Swaziland in effect had similar concessions thrust upon it. Hardly had these steps been taken, however, when they were overtaken by the onrush of political events.

In Basutoland a new constitutional commission proposed in 1963 that the country be granted self-government in 1964 and full independence in 1965. These proposals, after negotiation, have been accepted by Britain, and Basutoland will probably be the first of the three territories to achieve independence. Though the spectacle of a small, impoverished country beset by political dangers rushing headlong into independence may arouse apprehension elsewhere, the Basuto leaders themselves are optimistic. They are confident that the risks, which they recognize, are acceptable, especially if Britain can be persuaded to provide some insurance against the most threatening of them. They anticipate that Britain will buttress with financial grants the economic position of the country after independence, and hope that membership in the British Commonwealth will provide political protection against South African pressure.

One reassuring factor is the recognition, even by Basutoland's most ardent nationalists, of the need for understanding with their country's powerful neighbor. They have stated plainly their fundamental opposition to apartheid, but have been careful at the same time to express their desire for cooperation on economic matters of mutual interest with South Africa.

Quite obviously, independence for Basutoland is not a total or permanent solution. It can only be a way station to some new form of political association with South Africa, presumably after fundamental changes take place in that country. Independence, however, is now definitely at hand, and between that event and some eventual and larger political solution lies a hazardous existence over an indeterminate period of time. Once Basutoland is independent, internal political forces may well become more involved with and responsive to Pan-Africanist influences. Already the leadership, in anticipation of independence, has begun to reach out for ties with the independent African states to the north.

In Bechuanaland, likewise, important constitutional changes are brewing. In November 1963 leaders of the various political factions met to consider the next phase of constitutional development. They quickly reached agreement on a series of proposals to transform Bechuanaland into a self-governing, multiracial state, which means control by the African majority. These proposals have now been accepted by Britain. As the territory moves toward self-government, its relations with South Africa can only become more complicated. The Queen's Commissioner noted in November 1963 the increasingly stringent measures being applied by the South African government to control movement into and out of the High Commission Territories. At the same time he probably reflected the view of most Bechuana leaders in reaffirming that Bechuanaland would continue to give shelter to refugees arriving from South Africa. He counseled the Legislative Council, however, that the territory must pursue a policy of "caution but not timidity" toward those "neighboring countries who are so much stronger than ourselves but with whom we must trade to live."

Compared with attitudes in Basutoland, Bechuanaland's political mood is moderate. Seretse Khama, the Bamangwato chieftain who is likely to become the first prime minister, sees his country's role as one of proving to South African whites by example that races can work together effectively on a basis of equality, without harm to the interests of either. But other political elements, less sanguine about the prospects for changing white attitudes in the Republic, hope to make maximum use of Bechuanaland's strategic position as a corridor between independent Africa and South Africa. The British will remain in effective control for a brief period. Yet, within the next two to four years Bechuanaland is likely to become another new independent and unpredictable factor in the total situation in southern Africa.

The third of the High Commission Territories, Swaziland, is politically controlled by a combination of traditional tribal authority and influential whites. In 1963 the British imposed a new constitution because of the inability of a Swazi constitutional committee to reconcile its differences. In the election to the new Legislative Council held in 1964, conservatives and traditionalists prevailed, an outcome which for the time being at least blocks internal pressure for full independence as a multiracial state. The outcome of the election was an important gain for Dr. Verwoerd in his effort to achieve political accommodation with the territory. It is not impossible that Swazi traditionalists may yet join with whites in accepting for Swaziland something like Bantustan status within the South African embrace.

The South African Response

Since the creation of the Union, South Africa has repeatedly sought the incorporation of the High Commission Territories, and Britain has consistently met these overtures with delays, evasions, and rebuffs. For forty years South Africa appealed for the transfer on various grounds—as a reward for South Africa's services in two world wars, or as necessary to its defense, to its program for racial segregation, and to its plans for irrigation and economic development. As Afrikaner influence in politics increased, the tone of South African appeals for transfer of the territories became more peremptory, while British skepticism about apartheid intensified and resistance to the idea of transfer became more firm.

Since 1961, both parties have seemingly come to consider that the original agreement on eventual incorporation has lapsed. In 1963 Dr. Verwoerd stated in the House of Assembly that the question of incorporation was no longer "an active matter in the policy of the Republic." This is not to suggest, however, that South African interest in them has waned. On the contrary, it has become more intense while taking on a new tone and direction. As world opinion has progressively hardened against apartheid and as the international position of the Republic has grown more difficult, South Africa has begun to sense in the political developments in the territories grave threats—strategic, political, and psychological. It becomes increasingly concerned about what kind of "independence" they will have.

The possible emergence on its borders of multiracial, independent African states would inevitably lead to invidious comparisons between real and sham independence for black South Africans. Such political entities would not only challenge the assumptions of apartheid, but might provide a base for hostile political elements and invite the intrusion of Pan-African and Communist influence.

Disavowing any territorial ambitions, Dr. Verwoerd has since 1963 held out inducements to the territories to accept the status of "Bantu homelands," similar to that already accorded the Transkei area of South Africa itself, claiming that they would achieve "independence and economic prosperity far quicker and more efficiently" under South African tutelage. The reasons behind South Africa's interest are clear. The Bantustan plan gives primary importance to the preservation of traditional African authority or leaders; it rejects any conception of multiracial government; and it preserves for South Africa extensive powers in foreign relations, defense, and communications. Therefore, if Bantustan status were to be accepted by the territories, South Africa would expect to be able to control their political development, insure uniformity of native policy, prevent breaches in its national defense, and stabilize political relationships in the area. For such immense gains, which are not easy to distinguish from annexation, South Africa obviously would be prepared to pay a considerable price.

Interspersed with inducements, Dr. Verwoerd and other officials have spelled out with increasing clarity their readiness to use pressures of all kinds in the event the territories do not associate themselves with South Africa or that developments occur which South Africa would consider dangerous. In a report to the South African Parliament in January 1963, the Froneman Committee on Foreign Bantu estimated that half the foreign labor employed in the Republic (total: about 900,000) came from the High Commission Territories and recommended that the flow be drastically reduced. Barbed wire fences are said to be going up along the borders of the territories, and control of the movement of persons is being tightened. Afrikaner newspapers have played up the activities of agitators and political refugees in the territories and demanded strict control of such annoyances.

In its publicity the South African government continues to maintain the sunny view that the chances of good relations between the territories and the Republic will be greater after the former have achieved independence. According to that view, the granting of independence to the protectorates by Britain is in accordance with South Africa's policy of separate development, and this is said to be one of the main reasons why the latter no longer has any intention of seeking their incorporation into the Republic.

South Africa may possibly win favorable response to its proposals from traditional elements in Basutoland and Swaziland. But for the majority of Africans in the territories the Bantustan idea is unattractive. South Africa, therefore, is certain to be subject to increasing irritation, if not menace, by activities within and emanating from these areas. It will be confronted in the course of time with difficult choices concerning pressures and retaliation to be applied—choices which will affect not only the territories themselves but also much broader aspects of the Republic's international position. Those choices will be a clear test of South Africa's willingness to deal on an equal basis with independent African areas within its sphere of decisive influence.

British Dilemmas

The "legacy of colonialism" is usually considered in terms of the consequences of the past for the former colonies. But for the metropoles there has been a considerable legacy also. The process of disengagement from imperialism has not been without cost or hazard to Great Britain, and in the case of the High Commission Territories it has incurred a particularly troublesome and profitless set of continuing obligations.

In dealing with them Britain has demonstrated in rare fashion the qualities of a democratic government responsive to liberal opinion at home and conscious of its international responsibilities. In the process of decolonization Britain has been subjected in southern Africa, as elsewhere, to criticism from all sides—from political factions within the dependencies and from many segments of world opinion. In hindsight British policy in the High Commission Territories is indeed vulnerable to attack, particularly for neglect of their economic, social, and political development. But it must not be overlooked that from the beginning Britain's policy has been deeply influenced by moral as well as political and economic considerations, above all by a sense of responsibility for the well-being of the inhabitants.

As for the conditions under which the territories might be transferred to South Africa, Britain from the outset imposed upon itself two obligations. First, no such action would be taken without the House of Commons being informed; and second, the wishes of the natives would be carefully considered. Over the years Britain's resistance, based on principle, to the claims of South Africa has probably been counter to its own interests. In these terms the territories have been worthless to the British, who on the other hand have had and continue to have enormous economic and considerable, though decreasing, strategic interests in South Africa.

If today there is any prospect in the High Commission Territories for independence and freedom, it stems from the protection British policy has afforded over the years. Had Britain at any time reacted purely in terms of its direct economic and strategic interests, it would long since have turned them over to South Africa. Or, if it were now prepared to abandon broader obligations, it could simply accept their current demands for independence and be done with them. That Britain has not and will not follow either course is to the great advantage of all concerned. As accelerating political forces now drive the territories toward independence, however, Britain may well confront situations in which its responsibilities and interests are far greater than its effective power. For example, Basutoland, a self-governing but not yet completely independent area, might deliberately or inadvertently trigger an incident vis-à-vis South Africa requiring British interposition. In Bechuanaland political developments may occur which will provoke violent South African reaction and put important British interests in jeopardy.

Can Britain allow itself to be drawn into military conflict or economic warfare with South Africa over these remnants of empire? Can one expect Britain, whose economy is already laboring heavily, to provide growing infusions of technical and economic assistance to protect the fragile economies of the territories against suffocation? Will Britain, despite relentless criticism, continue to try to regulate the tempo of their constitutional evolution so as to lessen the hazards of political explosion? We may hope the British will be able to prevent serious crises from arising, and in the event will deal with them not purely in terms of narrow and immediate interest or of purely domestic political convenience. There are few other major powers about which such optimism would be justified.

Choices Before the United States

Direct American interests in the High Commission Territories are minimal. Equally minimal has been the influence of the United States upon their internal evolution. Nevertheless, because of their possible impact on the wider problems of the region, we cannot be indifferent to them.

As with other issues in southern Africa, the United States has to speak out if only because the subject has been brought before the United Nations. In the first U.N. action on the three territories in June 1962, the General Assembly adopted a resolution calling on the United Kingdom to accelerate constitutional development. The United States and Great Britain opposed the resolution as unnecessary and unrealistic. More recently, in December 1963, the Assembly passed another resolution regretting that the British had not yet implemented the previous one, calling for the restitution of alienated land within the territories, urging U.N. economic assistance, and declaring that any attempt to annex the areas or to encroach upon their territorial integrity would be regarded as an act of aggression and a violation of the Charter. On this occasion the United States abstained.

In the past the Organization of African Unity has not given great attention to the three territories but more recently has begun to take note of them. In the future they are likely to be more in the public eye, especially if they have their own voice through membership in the OAU and the United Nations. Their problems will then unavoidably, and perhaps usefully, become a matter of wider concern to the international community. Although their political emergence presents some hazards, it should probably be viewed as a healthy and desirable development. As they become more fully independent, they will increase political uncertainty in the region, but they may also clarify the issues raised by South African policy and provide a greater flexibility of policy to those trying to cope with the total situation.

The touchstone of American policy in the period immediately ahead should be acceptance of the movement of the three protectorates toward independence, but not in a manner or at a rate which would provoke the discharge of destructive political forces. It should also try to help maintain a reasonable degree of rapport between the territories and South Africa. Realistically, whatever political fate they may suffer or enjoy in the future, they must nonetheless live and function within the South African economic orbit. If their economic links with South Africa should be broken, the consequences in terms of human suffering for their populations would be grievous.

The United States should also accept the premise that no amount of economic assistance or of political protection which it can provide would be sufficient to insulate the areas from the consequences of any extreme and imprudent acts against South Africa. Indeed, if there is hope that the High Commission Territories will not contribute to political calamity in southern Africa as they advance toward independence, that hope is essentially dependent upon the moderation of their political leaders.

The United States can best serve its interests by joining its efforts to those of the United Kingdom, which basically are consistent with American concepts and objectives and are of vastly greater relevance and effect in the area itself. In supplementing British efforts the United States must be prepared to provide an increasing measure of economic and especially educational assistance, as well as to accept a degree of political commitment and cost, such as cooperating with Britain to discourage any encroachment on the territorial integrity of the areas or to guarantee their rights of access and egress across South African territory.

Washington has now wisely decided to station a diplomatic representative at Mbabane in Swaziland to maintain contact with all three territories. Because of the rapidly changing situations, it is of greater importance than ever that the United States be directly and currently informed of developments, especially since Chinese and Russian interest in the various areas of southern Africa has now sharpened.

Over the longer run it would seem advisable for the United States to begin consultation both with its Western allies, especially Great Britain, and with various African states to examine possibilities of some kind of federative solution to the problems of southern Africa, including the High Commission Territories. Until the political future of South Africa becomes clarified, it is impossible to determine what long-term political and economic solution for the territories might best serve their requirements. But it is not too early for serious thought on that very question.

Chapter VI

South West Africa

In the 1930s, in a remote and then little known part of the world, Ethiopia, the League of Nations was subjected to the ultimate test of its viability and effectiveness as an organ of collective security. In the 1960s, in an equally remote and little known area, South West Africa, the United Nations may meet a similar test.

In a legal case submitted by two former League members, Ethiopia, and Liberia, South Africa's administration of the territory of South West Africa is being challenged. Judgment by the International Court of Justice is anticipated in the latter part of 1965. Once the Court's judgment is handed down, a sequence of events will be set into motion which ultimately may bring to a head not only the snarled problem of South Africa's international responsibility in the administration of South West Africa, but also the future of the Court itself and possibly of the United Nations. The outcome of the case could also have very important implications for the issue of apartheid within South Africa. Without question, the South West Africa case is the most momentous the Court has ever considered. Its outcome, for better or worse, will provide a clear measure of the present state of international commitment to the principles of the rule of law and international responsibility under the U.N. system.

South West Africa is about the size of Texas. Strategically located in the southwestern corner of Africa, it has long common frontiers with South Africa, Bechuanaland and Angola, and touches on Zambia at the end of a narrow tongue of land, the Caprivi Strip. Its total population only slightly exceeds half a million people, of whom about 74,000 are white. Ninety per cent of the whites are citizens of South Africa. The African majority is divided into several distinct tribal groups.

Although the land is largely arid, there are areas in which agriculture and ranching are profitable. There is a small and thriving fishing industry, and the mineral resources of the country are considerable. Seven South African mining corporations are dominant in South West Africa, but British and American investors hold a substantial minority interest in all of them, and a controlling interest in one. Because of its resources and small population, it is potentially one of the more prosperous areas in Africa. Per capita income is among the highest in Africa, although the gap between white and non-white income is wide.

South Africa's policy of apartheid has to a large degree been applied in South West Africa, making the situation of the black African comparable to that of his counterpart in South Africa. By legislation his rights in landholding, freedom of movement, wages and employment, political life, and education have been severely limited. He has been relegated to a status of imposed and permanent inferiority. Because of greater poverty, lower level of education, and weaker African leadership, South West Africa is perhaps an instance of even more total exploitation and domination than South Africa itself.

Legal Status of the Territory

South West Africa, a German colony after 1884, was occupied by South African troops during World War I. At the Peace Conference, South Africa, supported by the British and French, proposed annexation of the territory. This was vehemently, and in the end successfully, opposed by President Woodrow Wilson. The result, to judge from the record, was that South Africa somewhat grudgingly undertook responsibility as mandatory for the territory. The Mandate was classed under the League of Nations covenant in group C, i.e., former German colonies which were least developed economically and politically. The primary obligation was that "the mandatory *shall promote to the utmost* the material and moral well-being and the social progress of the inhabitants of the Territory subject to the present Mandate." [1]

The League supervised the Mandate in three ways: first, annual reports had to be submitted to the Permanent Mandates Commission by the mandatory on its administration; second, the mandatory had to transmit petitions to the Council of the League, which could make recommendations; and third, the consent of the Council was required for any change in the terms of the Mandate. South Africa in practice viewed the Mandate as tantamount to annexation. General Smuts, Prime Minister of South Africa, was reported to have said, "In effect the relations between the South West Protectorate and the Union amount to annexation in all but name." [2]

The indigenous peoples of South West Africa hoped for a more enlightened administration under the Mandate, but in this they were soon disillusioned. Three punitive expeditions against as many tribes were conducted by South Africa in the first years. The country was quickly thrown open to white settlers, and in the succeeding years hundreds of large farms were allocated to incoming whites. Reserves were selected for the Africans in 1922, and segregationist policies were progressively applied thereafter.

During its life the League's Mandates Commission repeatedly criticized South Africa's reports, sometimes in harsh terms. But the League Council was without power to correct abuses. It could act only by unanimous consent, and South Africa was entitled to vote on issues involving its administration. Thus, during the interwar period, South Africa interpreted and administered its Mandate over South West Africa according to the principles and racial doctrines by which its own segregated society was governed.

At the end of World War II, under the new United Nations, the Mandate system was replaced by that of Trusteeship, which has similar but more explicit objectives and involves greater international accountability. South Africa's declared intention was to have South West Africa internationally recognized as an integral part of the Union. At the time a representative of South Africa significantly stated that "The Union Government will . . . regard the dissolution of the League as in no way diminishing its obligations

[1] Article 2 of the Mandate (emphasis added).
[2] *Cape Times*, September 18, 1920.

under the Mandate, which it will continue to discharge with the full and proper appreciation of its responsibilities until such time as other arrangements are agreed upon concerning the future status of the territory." [3] General Smuts, however, informed the United Nations of South Africa's hope to annex South West Africa, arguing that it was geographically and strategically a part of South Africa and economically dependent upon it, that its tribes were of the same racial origins, and that the large majority of its whites were South African nationals. He admitted that the ultimate objective of the Mandate and Trusteeship systems was eventual self-government and statehood, but he contended that for South West Africa, in view of its low economic potential and development, this aim was not practical. The argument was rejected, and the Assembly refused to approve annexation.

With the exception of South Africa, all the eight countries then holding mandates agreed to place their mandated territories under the Trusteeship system pursuant to Chapter XII of the U.N. Charter. South Africa, nevertheless, submitted a report on South West Africa to the General Assembly in 1947. In 1948 the Trusteeship Council criticized it, pointing out, among other things, that the "indigenous inhabitants of the Territory have no franchise, no eligibility to office and no representation. . . ." After that South Africa submitted no further reports, charging that they were being used as a means of bringing to task not only its administration of South West Africa but of South Africa as well. In effect, South Africa denied its obligations under the Mandate, which it insisted had expired with the demise of the League of Nations.

From 1946 on, numerous negotiations took place between South African representatives and various U.N. committees—but without positive results. The South African government would not enter into a trusteeship agreement for South West Africa, nor would it accept its international responsibilities for the territory, abide by its international accountability in submitting reports, or permit South West African petitioners to appear before U.N. commissions. At one point an Assembly committee took the extraordinary step of granting a hearing on an oral petition by the Reverend Michael

3 League of Nations, *Official Journal. Records of the . . . Twenty-first Ordinary Session of the Assembly* (Geneva, 1946), pp. 32–33.

Scott, representing the Herero chiefs, an action which caused the South African delegation to walk out of the meeting.

Between 1946 and 1960 more than sixty resolutions on South West Africa were passed by the General Assembly and various U.N. committees without significant effect in causing South Africa to change its position. In the same period, on three occasions, the Assembly appealed to the International Court of Justice for advisory opinions on the international status of South West Africa. In the first of these, the Court in 1950 made clear that South Africa's obligations under the Mandate had not lapsed with the end of the League. It concluded that the U.N. General Assembly was legally qualified to exercise the supervisory functions previously exercised by the League with regard to South West Africa, and that South Africa was obliged to submit to such supervision and control by the Assembly. Among other things, the Court also expressed its opinion (by a vote of 8 to 6) that although South Africa was not obliged to submit the territory to trusteeship, it could not unilaterally alter its legal status. In 1955 the Court advised that the United Nations could reach decisions regarding South West Africa by the two-thirds majority prescribed in the Charter rather than by unanimity, under the procedures of the League, as urged by South Africa. In its third opinion in 1956, the Court indicated that the Assembly's Committee on South West Africa could grant oral hearings to petitioners from the territory. Such rulings of the Court were not legally binding, however, and had no effect on the South African position.

Thus, for fifteen years a large proportion of the member states of the United Nations attempted by every consultative and persuasive means to cause South Africa to fulfill its international responsibilities in the administration of South West Africa. The result of this sustained effort, reflecting in part the widespread objection of member states to South Africa's racial policies, was only frustration.

Then in 1960 a most significant action was taken. At the second conference of independent African states held at Addis Ababa in June, a resolution was adopted urging that the obligations of South Africa concerning South West Africa be submitted to the International Court of Justice for adjudication in a contentious proceeding. This action was made possible by the fact that South Africa, under the terms of the Mandate by which it had assumed responsibility for South West Africa, had agreed to submit disputes concerning the Mandate to the League's Permanent Court.

Applications were filed with the Court in November 1960 in the names of Liberia and Ethiopia, two African states that had been members of the League at the time of its dissolution—a tactic adopted to avoid possible jurisdictional difficulties. The action was brought pursuant to a unanimous resolution of the independent African states of the Organization of African Unity.

The three main contentions of the applicants are: first, that apartheid is inconsistent with Article 2 of the Mandate, particularly the obligation to "promote to the utmost the material and moral well-being and the social progress of the inhabitants . . ."; second, that South Africa has disclaimed its accountability to the United Nations and no longer fulfills its responsibilities as a mandatory; and third, that South Africa has gone beyond its permitted authority in unilaterally changing the legal status of the territory. It should be noted that the Court has not been asked to recommend specific positive action; rather it has been asked to declare that certain policies of South Africa are inconsistent with the Mandate and that South Africa therefore has the duty to cease such policies. Nor is the Court asked to give legal authority for the transfer of the mandatory powers to the United Nations. The case has been carefully drawn to ask the Court to make certain findings of fact, to draw certain conclusions of law respecting violations of the Mandate and the obligations of the Mandatory, and to issue in effect what might be called a "cease and desist" order. The Court is not being asked for remedies which would necessarily involve it in deciding issues of a "political" character. Instead, it would appear that the essential purpose of the legal action is to lay the groundwork for subsequent political enforcement by the General Assembly or the Security Council in the event of a decision favorable to the applicants.

The applicants filed their brief on the merits of the case in the form of a so-called "memorial" in April of 1961. In its "counter-memorial" South Africa, as expected, contested the jurisdiction of the Court. The Court decided in December 1963 by an 8 to 7 vote that it had jurisdiction and was empowered to deal with the merits of the case. It so happened that every European judge on the Court, with the exception of the Russian, was among the seven dissenters. In the majority were the Latin American judges, the Chinese, the Egyptian, the Nigerian, the Russian and the American.

In defense of its position the South African government then filed an exhaustive study of the whole issue of apartheid, consisting of nine volumes and including some 1,500 pages of documentation. For the first time the doctrine and ideology of the policy have been given full and authoritative presentation. South Africa, by its decision not only to join issue on the merits of the case but to use the occasion for a detailed defense of its racial policy, has helped make the South West Africa case indirectly a trial before the world community of the doctrine of apartheid. And by its vigor and determination in attempting to maintain jurisdiction over South West Africa, the South African government has confirmed the impression that dangers and disorders of extreme gravity could develop within South Africa if independence or international control of South West Africa should occur.

The Timetable and the Alternatives

Decision by the Court is expected some time in the second half of 1965. It is, of course, possible that the Court may rule in favor of South Africa, but this is generally considered unlikely. Those who have followed the case closely and have studied the ruling of the Court on the jurisdictional issue believe that a verdict in favor of Liberia and Ethiopia will be given, probably by a wider margin than the preliminary judgment on jurisdiction. The year of decision is probably at hand, and it is a necessary task of statecraft to examine the probable consequences of the Court's action. The essential problem is more political than legal; and it is a rare and advantageous fact that in this case the world community can see the emergence of a crisis well in advance.

Interest in the consequences of the decision, assuming it to be favorable to Liberia and Ethiopia, will focus on two key points: (a) the enforcement actions to be sought by the complainants and the other Afro-Asian states before the Court or the political organs of the United Nations; (b) the reactions of South Africa to the Court's ruling and to the enforcement actions proposed.

If the Court rules for the applicants, and if South Africa fails to comply fully with the terms of the decision, they could ask the Council for enforcement procedures under Article 94 (2) of the Charter. This provides that the Security Council may "make recommendations or decide upon measures to be taken to give effect" to judgments of the Court. Alternatively, the applicants may appeal in the first instance to the General Assembly rather than to the Security Council. In the view of some observers, because of the hazards involved if Security Council enforcement action were invoked, the latter course would have many advantages.

As far as the Afro-Asian states are concerned, it appears probable that their response to a decision by the Court favorable to their position would aim at three objectives: (a) to terminate South Africa's Mandate over South West Africa and transfer its administration to the United Nations or some other trusteeship; (b) to prevent the case from being maneuvered back to the Court or to a slow-moving U.N. committee; and (c) to put the United States and the United Kingdom in a position where they will be obliged to take positive action against South Africa in defense of the principles of human rights and the Charter.

South Africa's Possible Response

In the event that South Africa is confronted with an unequivocal decision by the Court against its cause, it will be faced with a most difficult choice. Its reaction can only be surmised.

South Africa can defy the judgment and thereby the international community, with the possible consequence of political, economic, and conceivably even military sanctions being invoked to enforce the judgment and uphold the Court. It can comply with the ruling and thereby surrender not only a fundamental ideological position but also a degree of control over an area which it regards as of primary strategic importance. Or it can give "colorable compliance" without surrendering fundamental ideological and political positions in order to protract and obscure the matter for an indefinite period.

There are grounds on which to suppose that South Africa will flatly refuse to comply with an adverse ruling. The Verwoerd government has repeatedly expressed its defiance of the United Nations and of world opinion on apartheid. Sources reportedly close to Dr. Verwoerd have said that "if the Court rules against South Africa she will take South West Africa as India took Goa." On the other hand, there is not unimpressive evidence that South Africa is approaching the case in a fully responsible spirit, that it is in fact sensitive to the pressures of world opinion, and that it is clearly aware of the dangers in defying a Court ruling. It has not only not boycotted the Court case, but has fully participated in it.

The South African representative to the United Nations on at least one occasion has spoken in respectful terms of the Court and has declined under questioning to state that his government would refuse to accept its ruling in the South West Africa case. Moreover, some recent moves of the South African government can be interpreted as laying the groundwork for substantial concessions, if not complete acquiescence, to the Court's decision. Its action in holding in abeyance the application of certain of the recommendations of the Odendaal Commission may possibly reflect the existence of some flexibility and responsiveness in its policy beneath the rigidity of its present protestations.

In January 1964 Prime Minister Verwoerd presented to Parliament the report of a Commission of Inquiry into South West African Affairs (the Odendaal Commission). It proposed the division of South West Africa into twelve areas, ten of which were to be "homelands"—or Bantustans—for indigenous racial groups, who would have limited political rights within those areas. The report also contained ambitious recommendations regarding economic development, most of which would primarily benefit the whites, though some would result in benefits for Africans in the reserves.

The South African government, in the apparently serious belief that the report would win support from the international community, indicated that it would be promptly implemented. But response from many quarters was immediate and negative. To avoid a likely crisis in the United Nations, the United States joined with other Western governments in a forceful *démarche* to South Africa, warning that any attempt to apply the political aspects of the

Odendaal Report might well result in an interim Court order to South Africa to desist from an action prejudicial to a case *sub judice*. Rather than take that risk, Dr. Verwoerd, in a White Paper issued in April 1964, chose to put the political aspects of the plan in abeyance while moving forward on some of the economic proposals.

How such fragments of evidence of the South African attitude toward the Court add up is difficult to say. The immediate outcome, if the Court decides in favor of the applicants, may be a South African attempt to continue the fight on legal grounds, perhaps by seeking a clarification of the definition of compliance. The African states, on the other hand, will probably try to bring the situation to a prompt and definitive political decision, including withdrawal of the Mandate.

U.S. Policy Alternatives

Although blunted somewhat by an occasional inconsistency, American policy on South West Africa has from the beginning been exceptionally forthright. From about 1959 it began to diverge from that of some other members of NATO. In that year the General Assembly adopted a resolution calling upon the South African government to enter into negotiations either with the U.N. Committee on South West Africa or with any other committee the Assembly might appoint with a view to placing the territory under the international trusteeship system. The United States voted in the affirmative on this significant occasion even though all the Western European countries voted against or abstained.

Concurrently with this action the General Assembly, with the United States again voting in favor, adopted a resolution drawing the attention of member states to the legal steps open to them on South West Africa, namely the possibility of referring any dispute with the South African government over application of the Mandate to the International Court of Justice for adjudication. This resolution led directly to the decision taken at the 1960 Addis Ababa meeting of the African States to support the Ethiopian and Liberian suit.

If the American position has diverged from those of its European allies, the United States has not gone all the way over to the side of the Afro-Asian states. Since the initiation of the case before the International Court the United States has generally attempted to hold to the view that no action should be taken in the United Nations which would be prejudicial to the Court proceedings. On at least two crucial occasions the United States abstained on proposed resolutions in the United Nations, giving this argument as the basis of its position—and in consequence the United States has been subjected to considerable criticism by certain of the African and Asian states.

Despite its general position against U.N. action until the Court delivers its ruling, the United States has since 1960 voted affirmatively on a number of resolutions relating to South West Africa. In 1961, it voted for the strongest proposal yet formulated on the South West Africa question, a resolution urging the holding of general elections on the basis of universal adult suffrage; the repeal of all laws restricting freedom of movement, expression and association; the repeal of all apartheid laws; and the return of political refugees without risk of imprisonment or punishment. During the 1960–61 session the U.S. delegation charged that the policy of the South African government was out of place in the modern world where "tensions are likely to give rise to a general catastrophe and where all people demand the freedom to which they are entitled." Again in 1963, the U.S. delegation reiterated its position in favor of self-determination and its opposition to South Africa's attempts to annex South West Africa.

Thus, in a pattern now somewhat characteristic of American participation in the United Nations, U.S. representatives have invariably spoken in behalf of the principles of the Charter, but their votes in debates on South West Africa have not had the same consistency. In its day-by-day tactics the United States has attempted on the one hand to moderate the pressures of some of the African states and soften the tone of their resolutions, and on the other has urged South Africa and the Western European countries in the direction of compromise.

However effective or ineffective this line of conduct has been to date, the choices facing the United States become sharper and more costly in their implications as the moment of the Court decision approaches. Without question, the United States must pursue to the end the general decision it has already made to back the Court unequivocally. This could mean, in the ultimate instance, if the Court rules clearly for Ethiopia and Liberia and if South Africa should be unwise enough to refuse to comply with the judgment, the application of mandatory sanctions and even military measures to enforce it.

The hazards in such an eventuality are indeed grave. But the distinctions between the application of mandatory sanctions against South Africa because of its own racial policies, which was discussed in Chapter IV, and their application in the South West Africa case, are fundamental and controlling. At issue in the South African matter is the use of the ultimate powers of the United Nations to change an inflammatory, but nevertheless internal, situation within a member state. In the South West African case those powers would be invoked to enforce an international obligation and to uphold the Court and the concept of the rule of law in the world.

Support of the Court is an essential aspect of American support of the United Nations at a most difficult stage of its evolution. Any weakening in that support at this time would undercut the very foundations of American policy. The repercussions could affect the future of the Court, of the United Nations itself, and the stability of all of Africa. Recourse by the complainants to legal procedures has been regarded as consistent with the established American policy of favoring diplomatic, persuasive and legal means to resolve international disputes. U.S. representatives have repeatedly urged other member states to refrain from actions prejudicial to the litigation and the United States has indicated its own readiness to be guided by the Court's decision in future action on the South West Africa problem.

More broadly, the United States has frequently spoken out in support of the principle of the rule of law in international affairs. Although it reserves the right in cases in which this country is involved to determine whether a matter is solely within its domestic jurisdiction and therefore not justiciable by the Court, the United States has shown a strong interest in maintaining the general position and prestige of the Court. For instance, the United Nations has turned to the Court, with the active support of the United

States, in the matter of applying the rules of the Charter in case of nonpayment of assessments. The American position on this and other momentous matters would be compromised by any move undermining the authority of the Court.

To point out the essentiality of a clear and firm line of U.S. policy in support of the Court, however, is not to suggest that following such a policy will be an easy course. Although Article 94 of the Charter gives the Security Council a clear grant of power to "decide upon measures" to give effect to judgments of the Court, there remain grounds for legal argument whether this provision permits the use of military compulsion. Moreover, for enforcement action to be taken under this provision all permanent members of the Council would have to concur, a point which in turn may raise some interesting problems.

The Soviet Union as one of the permanent members would be in a curious position. It has never shown enthusiasm for the authority of the Court, for the legal approach to the resolution of international disputes, or for enforcement action, other than limited police actions, by the Security Council. However, because of the propaganda advantage to be reaped if blockage of enforcement could be laid at the door of the Western powers, the Soviet Union can be expected to show the greatest ingenuity in finding a way to reconcile its previous attitudes toward the Court with backing enforcement of the decision on the South West Africa case.

France, which to a considerable degree has withdrawn from responsible participation in collective action of the United Nations in recent years, would be another doubtful factor. And Britain would be in an especially painful position in voting for enforcement measures which could legally oblige it to impose economic sanctions on South Africa or possibly to support military action.

For the United States, compulsory enforcement measures would present relatively less serious difficulties, but the choice would still be far from easy. Even if the legal basis for action were established beyond question, political repercussions within the United States could be considerable. Many elements in American life which criticized support of the U.N. operation in the Congo would be aroused again and even more strongly. In addition, many responsible elements, although convinced of the legality of U.N. enforce-

ment action, would be disquieted by and resistant to any such ultimate use by the Security Council of its powers.

Because of the ominous implications of a showdown in the
United Nations over South West Africa, and in view of its uncertain outcome, it is of the highest importance that U.S. policy be
actively directed to averting such a confrontation. Otherwise, heavy
strains and possibly heavy losses to American interests might
have to be sustained—in domestic politics, within the Western alliance, in the stability and effectiveness of the United Nations, and
in relations with many countries of Africa. Nor can such a confrontation be avoided by yielding to the temptation merely to
ignore the issue, or by attempting to shelve it by recourse to the
Court in a new sequence of legal proceedings, or by relegating it
to a slow-moving U.N. committee. The pressures, emotions and national interests involved are so many and so powerful that such pro-
crastinating or diversionary tactics would most likely lead to an
eruption, rather than a dissipation, of the conflicting forces.

Therefore the United States would be well advised to proceed
simultaneously along several lines of action. First, in order to be
able wisely and firmly to hold to a line of policy following the
Court's ruling, it should look ahead to the political questions
which will arise once the legal issues have been adjudicated. It
can be assumed that the decision will not settle all the legal questions and that further litigation will be attempted, probably by
South Africa. Should the Afro-Asian states seek action (such as lifting the mandate) in the United Nations before these legal questions can be dealt with by the Court, it may be difficult for the
United States long to defer decision on such proposals on grounds
that the South West case remains *sub judice*. It is particularly important that the United States, the United Kingdom, and other
Western governments reach at least tentative agreement on their
responses to the various contingencies which may have to be
met. For example, should the United States support the immediate
lifting of the Mandate if the Court rules against South Africa?
And if so, should South West Africa then be given independence or placed under a trusteeship? If a trusteeship, should it be
single or multilateral? In turn, if the Mandate is to be lifted, the
United Nations would be well advised not to demand total sur-

render of a powerful and determined country like South Africa. What assurances and guarantees could and should be offered to South Africa to ensure that the area does not become a source of sabotage and danger on its borders? Should the United States in such circumstances support as a condition of trusteeship the total demilitarization of South West Africa? Or the granting to South Africa of inspection rights within the new trust territory?

Obviously, all the eventualities in the situation cannot be anticipated, nor should plans for such contingencies be frozen beforehand. But in a case such as this where the advent of a crisis is clearly discernible well in advance and where ultimately the United States may have to make major choices and commitments, anticipatory policy planning would seem to be both feasible and of positive value.

Second, the United States should make early and persistent efforts to persuade the South African government of the dangerous unwisdom of refusing compliance with the Court's order, including the clearest possible indication of the fact that the United States, if faced with the choice, will support enforcement of the Court's judgment with all appropriate means under the U.N. Charter.

Third, with equal forehandedness and vigor the United States should attempt to consult and collaborate with the more moderate and responsible African states concerning political actions to be taken after the Court's ruling. The object of such consultation cannot be merely to persuade the independent African states to dilute or postpone their demands for action. Rather, it must be to attempt to develop realistic lines of common action for evolutionary change of the constitutional status of South West Africa. In the interest of some degree of stability and evolutionary development in the whole southern part of the continent, it is especially important to the United States not to allow the African states to drift into a belief that their only means of countering Western delaying tactics is to propose more and more extreme and hasty measures for the independence of the territory.

There is some recognition among them that South West Africa is particularly unprepared to undertake full responsibility for the management of its own affairs in the near future. Nationalist political groups in the territory are divided along both tribal and party lines, and personal rivalries have led to much internecine conflict. The political inexperience of the inhabitants and their fearfully low level of educational and economic development have made the country less able than most other African areas to assume self-government. Therefore, it would seem quite possible for the United States, on the basis of positive proposals for the evolutionary constitutional development of the territory, to enlist the support of a good many independent African states for a trusteeship arrangement involving a reasonable transitional period.

Fourth, close and continuing consultation and cooperation between the United States and the United Kingdom in future actions on South West Africa should cover short-term measures (such as the effective joint action taken on the Odendaal Report), clarification of medium-term objectives (such as lines of argument to be taken with South Africa prior to the Court's decision), and longer-term efforts (such as political solutions to be proposed if South Africa's Mandate is lifted).

Over and beyond anticipatory actions to cope with the consequences of the Court's ruling, the United States should move to protect its long-term interests. At present the great bulk of South West Africans who receive advanced education relevant to the future leadership of the country are being trained in the Soviet Union or China. According to the best figures which have been gathered, it appears that only one in ten of the handful of political refugees or exiles who have left South West Africa is being trained in the United States or other Western countries. At an appropriate time the United States might therefore well demonstrate its positive concept of international responsibility by taking the lead in proposing expanded plans for the general economic, educational and social development of the area.

The South West Africa case may be, as some have said, the Achilles heel of apartheid. It could also be the Achilles heel of the International Court, of the United Nations, and of the concepts of the rule of law and of human rights under the United Nations Charter. It is a historic coincidence that at the same time that the United States through its Supreme Court has attempted to deal by legal action with its most sensitive and aggravated domestic social issue, race relations, a ground-breaking case concerning human rights is before the International Court of Justice. The South West Africa case at the international level may be of a significance equal to that of the Brown case in the history of the United States Supreme Court. If the Court rules in favor of the complainants, it will be a landmark in the extension of international law in the field of human rights and international responsibility.

The fact that these basic issues are being contested within a legal framework may help make it possible to translate great visions and concepts into reality, or it could lead to their being mired in meaninglessness and disillusionment. Given the racial overtones of a number of the international problems facing the United States today—e.g., the struggle in the Congo, the admission of Communist China to the United Nations, and the war in Viet-Nam—the outcome of the South West Africa case will affect matters in many parts of the earth.

Chapter VII

Conclusions

Southern Africa is a region under siege by all the forces of revolutionary change which characterize the contemporary world. The political changes which may occur will involve not minor alterations of policy but basic constitutional modifications and the eventual transfer of authority to black majorities. These are likely to be accompanied by still deeper alterations in the ways of life of the people, in their relations with one another, and in the patterns of social organization. In this simple and even obvious fact—the imminence and the probability of change—lies the kernel of the problem of American policy. Here is no stable political landscape in which the task of diplomacy is merely to adjust through negotiation points of friction or conflict between durable regimes. Rather it is a panorama of pressures and of movement, developing at varying rates of speed within the several areas, to which U.S. policy must relate and upon which it may be able to exercise some influence.

In short, the problem which southern Africa presents to American policy and diplomacy is the shaping of change. There may be areas in the world where American influence is so great that without pretention we could designate our role as one of exercising "the leadership of change," just as there may be areas so remote from American interest or impervious to our influence that the guiding line can only be to accommodate our policy to change. In southern Africa, though the United States cannot reasonably hope to control the evolution of events and should play essentially a secondary role, neither can it in prudence merely allow them to take whatever course internal or other external pressures may produce. But how to help shape their course and what American commitment is required or justified are complex questions to which prior experience provides no key.

The Direction and Rate of Change

The thrust and direction of change in southern Africa is unmistakably clear: gropingly but steadily the peoples are awakening to the possibility of modernizing their societies, improving their living conditions, and establishing government on the basis of consent of the governed. Given the racial composition of the countries of the area, the broad movement will be in the direction of majority control and the displacement of present white governments. The movement does not proceed evenly or continuously. But behind it are inexorable driving forces: the impact of Western concepts of democracy and human rights, the resentment of poverty, the stimulative effects of modern communications, the growth of race consciousness, the repercussions of the worldwide conflicts between the Western and Communist countries and within the riven household of communism itself.

Perhaps nothing in politics or international affairs is inevitable. But for the black majorities of southern Africa not to assume eventual control of their governments the whole course of contemporary history would have to be diverted and the deep forces underlying it would have to lose their momentum. In brief, government without the consent of the governed anywhere in southern Africa over the longer term, if not the shorter term, is almost certainly doomed.

Clear though the direction of change may be, its timetable remains impossible to predict. And the timing of change—whether five years or fifty—can have profound significance for policy. There are reasons to think the pace might be quite rapid. Even within the coming two or three years Basutoland, Bechuanaland, perhaps South West Africa, and possibly Rhodesia may pass to majority African control or may be set irrevocably on that road. Thus, broad streaks and patches of African control may break up the region's present homogeneity—with consequent effects upon the strategic, political, and psychological position of the remaining zones of white control.

By simple physical analogy it might be concluded that as the major mass is broken into smaller segments and as the total surface exposed to solvent political forces increases, resistance in the remaining areas of white control will dissolve at a more rapid rate. This could well happen. The pace of political change in Africa has often been underestimated in the past. The possibility cannot be overlooked that the political problems of southern Africa will shortly come to crisis and that in a crescendo the full restitution of the African continent to the control of its overwhelmingly black population will be accomplished.

It is not impossible, however, that this climax will not be reached for another twenty-five years or longer. The rapid political transformation of Africa since 1950 has required a remarkable confluence of forces, particularly a large degree of willingness on the part of the controlling European powers to give Africa back to the Africans. But in three citadels of white minority control which the Africans now seek to capture, the factors of metropolitan indifference or reasonableness or liberalism which were decisive in most of the northern and tropical areas are no longer present. It is conceivable, even probable, that Portugal and South Africa will bring to bear the last measure of military and financial strength at their disposal to try to maintain the present pattern of minority control—and such effort may prevail, at least for a number of years. The white governments in southern Africa have hardly begun to exploit the possibilities open to them for coordinated action in defense of their position and for shifting to the offensive.

It is by no means certain, moreover, that in all areas effective internal pressures against white minority control will be organized and sustained. The black populations reflect markedly differing levels of political development and unity. In some countries, political awareness appears to be widespread and there is great willingness to make personal and other sacrifices in order to force constitutional change; in others there is a high degree of political ignorance and indifference. In some countries the leadership of black nationalist movements is increasingly broken by imprisonment, exile and even death; in others, it has been unduly weak or has been rendered impotent by tribal division and factional dispute.

A singular aspect of the situation is the great importance of external forces. Of these, three are crucial: the independent African states to the north; the United Nations, with its overwhelmingly anticolonial majority; and the world Communist movement, including both of its now separate branches, Russian and Chinese.

Role of the Independent African States

There is no question of the serious concern of the independent African states about white minority control in the south, for it is rooted in deep resentments. The more sophisticated political figures are convinced that so long as any major portion of the continent remains under white control, the independence and security of the whole continent is endangered. There is thus every reason to believe that they will feel impelled to exert themselves relentlessly in behalf of displacing the present white regimes, using primarily the two instrumentalities available to them, the United Nations and their own Organization for African Unity.

In the United Nations the African states have developed techniques of extraordinary effectiveness in advancing their common objectives. Despite the weakness and instability of some of the regimes, African leaders have conducted a complex and unusual diplomacy drawing upon moral and symbolic elements, taking advantage of conflicts among the great powers, and exploiting the high purposes of the United Nations as well as the contradictions built into its structure.

It is likely that they will move from generalized pressures in the form of criticism and declarations to proposals for specific actions, voluntary or compulsory, to bring about the changes they seek. Such efforts through the United Nations are in a sense cost-free to the African states: the measures which they press on the major powers or the undertakings into which they hope to force the United Nations ultimately involve expenditures, sacrifices, and to a large extent risks which others, not the African states themselves, must bear. By its structure the world organization does not constrain them to moderation. In their determination to force change they may well make unrealistic demands upon the major powers and impose severe strains on the United Nations itself.

On their continent the new African states have made general though somewhat intermittent progress in evolving a measure of functional unity. Such unity was neither inevitable nor easy to achieve, considering the insane network of national boundaries they inherited from the colonial period and their naturally divergent interests and viewpoints on many issues. In spite of these difficulties, the Organization of African Unity, since its creation in 1963 at Addis Ababa, has considerably clarified and strengthened its program and structure. Recent developments in the Congo and growing internal strains of many of the member states have reopened old splits and produced a tendency to impetuosity of action. Whether the outstandingly able Guinean, Diallo Telli, who has been named as Administrative Secretary-General of the OAU, will be able to restore and develop the organization's unity and effectiveness remains to be seen.

Through the OAU, in contrast to the United Nations, the African states are both more free and more restricted in what they may do. They are free, for example, to furnish material help to the liberation movements of the south and to impose their own sanctions upon the Portuguese areas and South Africa. Yet they are more restricted in the sense that they themselves will be called upon to bear directly the costs and the risks of any actions decided upon. This paradox is already manifest in the actions which the OAU has taken. As in any alliance, the members have shown themselves far more ready to join in general declarations than in the actual contribution of money or material to the southern liberation movements or in the enforcement of boycotts. This is not a matter of hypocrisy, because a number of African states have taken measures of relatively heavy cost in imposing economic measures on South Africa and Portugal. But it does reflect a growing awareness of the real limits upon their resources and thus upon their power to force changes in southern Africa.

The independent African states may be expected to give increasing direct help to the nationalist movements and to seek means to impose economic disadvantage on the white minority governments without subjecting themselves at the same time to insupportable costs. In particular, they will strive to force the Western countries and their private investors to make political and economic choices between independent Africa and the white governments of southern Africa, to restrict their freedom to carry on trade, investment and military cooperation with both areas simultaneously. But all these efforts are likely to be kept within realistic bounds, determined not only by limited resources of the OAU member states but also by the restraint of the governments closest to the Battleline and hence most vulnerable to the repercussions of any action taken. This is not to imply that vituperative statements will cease; they may even be intensified. But the actions are likely to be much less drastic than the pronouncements. Whether or not even the present degree of moderation of African political leaders will persist depends, of course, on the degree of political instability in their own countries, the rate of political change in southern Africa, and, a very important factor, the extent and nature of Communist intervention.

The Soviet Union and Communist China

Communism is unlikely to be a determinant force in those parts of southern Africa where a dialogue is now in progress, as in the High Commission Territories, or where powerful international pressure is already causing movement, as in South West Africa. But where the dialogue has been interrupted, as in South Africa, or where it has never begun, as in Angola and Mozambique, further political change is likely to depend on the use of revolutionary methods and arms. There the opportunity is offered to both the Russians and the Chinese to extend their penetration and control by supporting violent and revolutionary elements. Both have declared their intention to support the anticolonial struggle and "wars of national liberation." The question is whether they consider the opportunities important enough for the advancement of their major interests to justify the political and financial costs involved.

The Soviets moved quickly in the wake of independence in Africa to give recognition and economic assistance to a number of the new states. These first efforts to a considerable extent ended in failure because of their own inexperience and heavy-handed-ness. From these mistakes, however, the Russians learned some lessons, and in recent months a second round of the drive appears to have begun. In contrast to the more radical tactics of the Chinese, and with far greater resources at their disposal, the Russians appear to be trying to win over the nationalist governments rather than to promote immediate Communist revolutions.

The Chinese have repeatedly said they consider Africa, along with Asia and Latin America, to be the areas where an "objective revolutionary situation" exists and the anti-imperialist struggle is decisive for the world-wide victory of communism. Chinese efforts, though getting a later start than those of the Soviet Union, have developed rapidly and dramatically. The first moves were directed at gaining diplomatic recognition, and these have been crowned with considerable success. In 1960 Communist China had been recognized by only two African states, the U.A.R. and the Sudan. By 1964, however, it had won recognition from seventeen. It had also begun to experiment with economic assistance, mainly for small, specific projects involving limited financial commitment and the promise of quick results. These have generally been well received.

In late 1963 and early 1964 Chou En-lai, with a sixty-man entourage, visited ten African countries. In addition to the goodwill and diplomatic objectives of his visit, a first-hand evaluation of Chinese efforts in Africa up to that point was made. Following his visit three new tendencies in Chinese policy have emerged: a willingness to make substantial commitments of aid in politically strategic areas; direct involvement in revolutionary activities within the independent African states; and even greater emphasis on special training and travel for young persons of high political potential, especially from the southern areas.

To some degree Russian and Chinese objectives in Africa coincide: to discredit the Western powers; to accelerate the disengagement of Africa from close ties with or dependence upon the West; to underscore Communist identification with anticolonial struggles throughout the world; and to strengthen the ties of the Communist world with the underdeveloped and non-white areas. But in significant ways their objectives differ, reflecting their bitter struggle for leadership of the world Communist movement. Indeed, it appears that their competition is an all-out political war in which no quarter will be asked or given.

In Africa, China is moving to the attack after having scored important gains against the Soviet Union in Asia. The attack has been geared to exploit Soviet weaknesses and to couple the Soviet Union with the Western powers as imperialists. Chinese representatives hammer on the theme that the Soviets through their economic assistance seek to dictate to the Africans, and they draw a sharp distinction between alleged Soviet practices and Chinese methods of cooperation. The Chinese likewise attempt to identify themselves with the backward nations, emphasizing the parallels between their problems and those which China has faced. They exploit carefully but unmistakably the factor of race and color to the disadvantage of the Russians.

The Chinese thrust poses a vexatious dilemma for the Russians. For a number of reasons it may be supposed that the latter do not seek to become heavily involved in additional disorderly and dangerous situations around the world at the present time. Moreover, for Soviet propaganda purposes, there are definite advantages in permitting the ugly race problem of South Africa, for example, to remain a running sore for years rather than to bring it to a head. On the other hand, it seems doubtful that in a situation as powerfully symbolic as that of southern Africa the Soviet Union can allow itself to be pushed into the background by the Chinese by failing to match or outmatch the assistance and the extremism of China in support of revolution and "liberation." On balance, therefore, southern Africa is likely to become increasingly a focus of Communist interest, both Russian and Chinese, and Communist support for violence will grow as the area becomes a center of turbulence and danger commanding world attention.

For the leaders of independent Africa the growing intrusion of communism and the Sino-Soviet conflict in their continent arouses mixed feelings. They are keenly aware of the struggle which is developing on their soil and are alert to its implications not only for southern Africa but for independent Africa as well. Yet it is unlikely that they can lay any powerfully restraining hand on Soviet or Chinese efforts. The leaders of independent African governments can hardly oppose revolutionary moves, even if Communist-supported, to bring down white minority regimes. If the Soviets and Chinese have a great interest in taking the vanguard position in the liberation of southern Africa, the African states have an equal and even greater interest in seizing and holding such leadership for themselves, partly because of their determination to keep the continent free from compromising entanglements with external powers.

Guidelines for American Policy in Southern Africa

The primary task of American diplomacy in southern Africa, as already stated, is to seek to influence the process and direction of change. To do so will require unusual clarity about the eventual goal toward which our efforts are directed, an unusual degree of flexibility and adaptability in pursuing that goal, and, above all, a shift from traditional and essentially static concepts of diplomacy to an approach as new and dynamic in its way as the Marshall Plan was for Europe in 1947.

The fundamental U.S. commitment should be to assist and encourage political change in the direction of majority rule and self-government. Without insisting on conformity to specific institutions or forms, the United States should identify itself constantly and unequivocally with the broad principles of self-determination, political rights and social justice. It must do so because such a course is right and because it is realistic. No other objective is consonant with the nature of American society and government; no other objective is consonant with the general movement of current history. In the short and medium term, that course may disturb the appearance of stability under repressive regimes; but over the longer term there is no alternative which offers a greater chance of governments being accepted as legitimate and therefore with a prospect of permanence.

In pursuing such an objective, however, the United States obviously has to take into account not only the urgencies and dangers in southern Africa but also the larger background of the world situation and of the several major present dangers to peace, of which southern Africa is only one. As a broad guide to policy this means that the United States should seek to accomplish its objectives in southern Africa by the consistent and active application of persuasion and influence; but it must also, to the ultimate degree of practicality, refrain from taking part in any effort to resolve problems by force.

There is no final assurance that persuasive efforts will be sufficient; and certainly halfhearted or confused efforts to apply persuasion and pressure will be ineffective. Nonetheless, the United States should continue to use and support the use of peaceful measures insofar as possible. By their very nature the political and social problems of southern Africa are rooted in conflicting attitudes and contrasting traditions of the white and non-white communities. If viable solutions to these intractable problems are to be found without sacrificing the rights and position of either majority or minority, they can be found only through communication, consultation and compromise. Solutions imposed by force, in these circumstances, particularly by external force, can be neither just nor durable.

Not only must the United States view the problems of southern Africa in a world perspective, but it should also recognize fully the limits of its power and influence in dealing with them. If the United States forbids itself the direct use of its military power to force change in southern Africa—as it intelligently and responsibly must—then its remaining capacity to influence the situation is relatively limited. In a curious fashion southern Africa may represent the kind of international problem in which the potential dangers to American interest are far greater than the acceptably available powers of the United States to deal with them. In practical policy terms this means that if the United States is to protect its interests there, it must join its influence to that of other powers sharing its general objectives. Joint effort is therefore an absolute requirement of American policy.

The United Nations offers one important medium for such collaboration. To an abnormal and regrettable degree, U.N. discussions about southern Africa have centered on sanctions, with their implicit negativism. But there is need for the United States, the United Kingdom and others to give more attention to possible constructive collective measures—not only to sanctions which are but one specific form. However, to rely exclusively on collaboration through the United Nations presents many difficulties. Cooperation outside the United Nations with allies or groups of selected countries can in certain situations offer many advantages of flexibility and acceptability.

First and foremost, this means continued and increasingly effective collaboration with Great Britain. In the High Commission Territories, Rhodesia, South West Africa and South Africa, Britain is the most decisive single external influence. The United States should therefore seek to construct the closest possible working partnership to develop plans and initiatives with Great Britain.

Moreover, significant possibilities exist for cooperation between the United States and various countries of Western Europe in regard to southern Africa. In over-all political policy, the coordination of economic and educational assistance, and the planning and execution of specific diplomatic *démarches,* it would seem of great value to the United States to try to develop new patterns of collaboration with individual Western European powers and with groups of them, such as those associated in the Common Market.

In addition, there is need for active American cooperation and collaboration with the independent nations of Africa. From the point of merely counselling them to be patient and to be anti-Communist, American policy has moved to a recognition and acceptance of their presence as fully constituted national entities on the world scene. But to a large extent, the United States has not yet appeared ready to accept the new African states as collaborators or to take their leaders quite seriously in joint consultation; and it has been elaborately cautious in encouraging their participation in multilateral enterprises. These states can be of great usefulness in southern Africa. They can be encouraged in the direction of moderation and responsibility by giving them a larger stake in the work of the international community and by carefully involving them in joint undertakings.

The foregoing suggestions covering objectives and guidelines for U.S. policy have included no reference to the obvious and important question of precluding Communist penetration or political control by either the Soviet Union or China. The hazards of such an eventuality are self-evident. If international Communist elements can direct the political and racial struggles of the area, the benefits for their worldwide influence would be enormous. In more material terms the great wealth of South Africa, if brought under the control of a Communist government, could change the political coloration of much of Africa.

Precluding Communist influence in southern Africa, however, must be a derivative rather than a direct goal of U.S. policy. No clearer case of the sterility of a purely negative anti-Communist approach can be found. Either the United States will succeed through the vigor and effectiveness of its constructive efforts in accelerating progress toward self-determination and majority control in southern Africa—the only real chance of blocking Communist influence—or it will be left with only three alternatives, all disagreeable and damaging: (a) it could, in the face of growing racial strife and violence, merely do nothing, that is, resign itself to the inevitability of widening Communist influence in the areas; (b) it could join with white racist governments in a joint effort to fight black African political advance, a course bound to throw all Africa into the arms of the Communists and to undercut the spiritual and political basis of American leadership of the free world; (c) it could take a line paralleling that of China or Russia in violent and revolutionary assault on white resistance, a course perhaps preferable to the others but obviously dangerous and acceptable only under extreme necessity.

Beyond clarity of objective, flexibility and perspective, the problems of southern Africa impose on the United States an even deeper requirement, the re-examination of some basic concepts underlying traditional American diplomacy.

Diplomacy in various historic periods has undergone shifts in its mission and style; it has marched ashore with the troops as well as danced at the court. In southern Africa U.S. diplomacy is confronted with the need to adapt itself to a swift-moving, revolutionary scene. It must face the task of protecting and advancing the national interest not primarily by the usual processes of negotiation and communication with stabilized states, but rather through developing contact with and exerting influence upon powerful but still largely inchoate political forces in areas where new nations are in the trauma of birth. These new and dynamic requirements have been effectively stated by former Deputy Under

Secretary of State, U. Alexis Johnson: "The first [role] is to assure the freedom of the revolution. We must prevent external interference, subversion and aggression from stifling the revolutionary process. The second is to give such cooperation and support as we can to the orderly social, economic and political development of the emerging nations." [1]

Thus, in southern Africa American diplomacy is confronted with a triple task: first, to develop contact and communication with those political groups presently not in control of government but likely to assume control in the future, in order to exert some influence on the character of the regimes they will establish; second, during the period of political transformation, to attempt to "assure the freedom of the revolution" by helping to reduce or counter those internal or external factors which could frustrate evolutionary change and lead to violence and disruption; and third, during this hazardous and inflamed transitional stage nonetheless to attempt to maintain workable relations with existing regimes in order to assist transition and to protect current American interests and objectives.

This definition of the diplomatic task puts notions of sovereignty, protocol, nonintervention, and many other familiar considerations into a radically different framework. It has little in common with the traditional diplomacy, of which Sir Harold Nicolson has given the classic exposition. It extends the field of diplomatic action far beyond government-to-government relations to include persons and groups not only not participants in existing regimes but even outlawed by them. It is a definition of diplomacy which stresses the nature and the tempo of change, the objectives toward which change is moving, and the national interest in contact with all the principal elements involved in the process of change. It implies, therefore, a diplomacy which operates on several levels simultaneously. It treats sovereignty as more of an eventual than an actual reality and it requires involvement in what once was considered to be the internal political processes of other nations. It is therefore unorthodox, full of hazards—and yet inescapable. Until our basic diplomatic concepts are shifted to acceptance of such strange new

[1] *Department of State Bulletin,* January 8, 1962.

realities, it is likely that the subconscious wish to return to the womb of "proper diplomacy" will lead American practice to a preference for the familiar as against the unfamiliar, the dignified as against the disorderly, the *de jure* as against the *de facto,* and the old against the new—all of which in a situation like that of southern Africa may be seriously and enduringly damaging to our national interest.

The Diplomatic Instrumentalities Relevant to Change

Dynamic definition of the diplomatic mission in an area like southern Africa also throws emphasis upon the new and most controversial elements in the armory of diplomacy—including economic assistance, cultural and educational programs, informational and propaganda efforts, covert activities, the work of private American organizations abroad—and the United Nations itself. In pragmatic response to obvious needs in the postwar period, the United States has rapidly expanded its expenditures for these newer kinds of international activity. But their expansion has not been accompanied by a parallel development of concepts for their employment and their coordination. The common and essential quality of these instrumentalities is that they are means by which to influence economic and political change, which in turn is the central problem of diplomacy in tomorrow's world.

In the United Nations, for example, the United States has at times shown ineptness in dealing with the intangible and symbolic factors which so often form the substance of U.N. debates. The activities which take place there differ markedly in character from the usual diplomatic conference. To approach the complex problem of U.S. representation before that body as if it called primarily for the exercise of traditional diplomatic skills and methods is to overlook the unique opportunity it presents. The distinctive, even bizarre aspects of the United Nations as a diplomatic setting are many. States debate issues in which they are not materially concerned and for which they have no responsibility; the voting power and influence of the participants is not correlated with their industrial, military or even moral power; the agreements reached frequently carry no effective means for their enforcement. Yet those debates and discussions—however confused or even irresponsible on occasion they may have been—are a mirror held up to the concerns and attitudes of the world. Words spoken at the United Nations, resolutions adopted by it, and ideas propagated through its organs are disseminated throughout the world, reaching mass audiences everywhere. What goes on at the United Nations, therefore, has an importance not only for the specific matters under debate but also for world opinion and the climate of international relations.

Although the United Nations has been a feature of the world scene for nearly twenty years, the United States has only begun to understand the means for adapting diplomatic methods to its special setting. American diplomacy apparently still finds it difficult to reconcile traditional diplomatic or parliamentary criteria of orderliness and responsibility with the flux, intensity and intangibility of actions at the United Nations. A thorough re-examination of the patterns of American conduct there might possibly reveal an undue emphasis on legalism and formalism. It might also open up possibilities by which the United States, while retaining a responsible posture, could extricate itself from the catatonic attitude which has been its trademark in past years in dealing with most issues in the field of human rights and in southern Africa.

A second area in which to sharpen concepts and therefore the effectiveness of our instrumentalities is that of foreign economic assistance. As U.S. foreign aid programs have shifted their focus from Western Europe to the less developed areas of the world, we have slowly achieved a more sophisticated understanding of the requirements for modernizing primitive societies. In southern Africa, however, much of what has been learned in other underdeveloped regions does not apply. For example, in the independent underdeveloped countries increasing stress is given in our aid programs to requiring "maximum self-help" and "demonstration of significant progress in development." But in areas like Angola and Mozambique such requirements make little sense because the vast majority of the population has no voice in the government and therefore has no reason to make special efforts for economic development which would benefit essentially a controlling white minority.

Similarly, in areas like Bechuanaland and Basutoland, the notion that aid can be short-term support until the country reaches "take off" is almost irrelevant. These are extremely backward areas with a meager base of economic resources and still more meager resources of human skills. If the take-off stage can ever be reached, it will be a very long-term affair involving the transformation of the economic and social structures as well as solution of the political problems of the entire region.

Thus, in southern Africa, economic aid should not be seen primarily as an instrument for achieving economic objectives. Since political settlements are the precondition to any stability or development, economic aid in the period ahead might be employed essentially as a means of facilitating such political settlements. How could economic aid in Rhodesia, for example, be used to accelerate the process of enfranchising the black majority? Is there any possibility of trading economic assistance in Angola and Mozambique for agreement in principle by Portugal to eventual self-determination? To what extent can U.S. aid in the High Commission Territories be used to encourage their new black-controlled governments to follow policies of prudence and realism in dealing with South Africa, and in turn to protect them from disruptive pressure or penetration from South Africa? How could economic assistance in South West Africa be used during an interim period of United Nations trusteeship to accelerate the preparation of the country for handling its own affairs? To enable American officials freely and fully to use aid funds to deal with such political questions, much present practice, theory, and legislation would have to be overhauled. The more incisive employment of U.S. economic power and assistance to advance foreign political objectives is uncharted and risky territory. But President Johnson has indicated his readiness in connection with Viet-Nam to use economic assistance as an inducement to political settlement. Such an approach might have wide application in southern Africa.

A third area in which American thinking and practice could be sharpened is that of cultural and educational exchange, a growing although still minor aspect of U.S. foreign policy and programs. In southern Africa such activities rank very high among those available and useful to the U.S. government. They offer the principal available means for establishing a bridge of contact with the various elements of the emerging nationalist movements, the first of the triple tasks of American diplomacy in the area as suggested earlier. To date, however, U.S. cultural and educational programs have been conducted on a small scale and without benefit of a clear framework of political considerations. In contrast, the Russians and Chinese are now conducting such activity with persons from southern Africa on a substantial scale. Their concentration on agitational and military training reflects their theoretical expectations of the probable stages of revolutionary development in the area.

For the effectiveness of our cultural and exchange programs in southern Africa, systematic analysis of the objectives sought and the techniques to be used will prove most valuable. In many parts of the world, educational and cultural programs have been devoted broadly and sometimes loosely to "building understanding and friendship" between nations. But the United States has already discovered that merely facilitating and encouraging the interflow of scholars and informational materials is often unproductive and possibly negative in its effects, especially when the foreign partner involved is a totalitarian regime which can systematically divert and exploit such interchange to its own advantage.

To make such programs productive we have to cope with conceptual and operational problems which are unique. For the United States to attempt to broaden "free" cultural and educational exchanges with South Africa, Angola or Mozambique would accomplish no positive purpose for the long run, and in fact would have the negative effect of identifying the United States with reaction and offensive racial policies. Creative thought needs to be given to the scale of such activity required in southern Africa, the methods of recruitment and selection of students, the nature of the training to be offered, the categories of leadership which should be given priority, the methods by which continuing contact with young leaders can be maintained after the exchange, and the utility of private, nongovernmental institutions in carrying out such programs. Until this is done, one of the most promising instrumentalities available to the United States will continue to be used in an erratic, undirected and somewhat unproductive fashion.

The pragmatic and flexible American approach in creating and using its newer tools of foreign policy has many advantages. Yet improvisation, an absence of general concepts, and lack of coordination have been carried to a point where effectiveness has been seriously reduced. Washington has tried in various ways in the postwar period to improve what has been called "operations coordination" in the broad area of foreign policy, generally with discouraging results. The most prominent effort in this direction, namely the Operations Coordination Board created under the Eisenhower administration, was promptly dismantled when President Kennedy took office, and responsibility for its functions was transferred to the State Department. It is not yet clear that the change has markedly improved the situation.

Nor, given the enormous scale and complexity of the U.S. government, is it likely that any easy solutions can be discovered. But in discussing the problem of relating American diplomacy and foreign policy to the circumstances and requirements of the revolutionary parts of the world, in analyzing and employing more effectively the newer instrumentalities of policy, and in considering the interrelationship of these various elements, we are discussing the core issues of the modernization of American foreign policy.

Southern Africa is virtually a synthesis and a symbol of the most tangled problems confronting American diplomacy. It is a situation of revolutionary politics more than of traditional diplomatic relationships, heavy with intangibles and light in the traditional elements of direct American economic and military interests. It calls for the employment of new and as yet little understood instruments of total diplomacy and for private as well as official action. It is a problem in which anticipatory measures can produce major returns, whereas reactive policy is likely to be costly and fruitless. It can best be dealt with through collaboration and consultation with other governments and not independently. On all these counts it strikes U.S. foreign policy and practice at points of vulnerability.

It therefore lays upon the U.S. Department of State the extremely heavy responsibility of formulating and conducting a distinctive line of foreign policy, one which is bound to be difficult to carry through. Given the nature of our democratic society, the task becomes all the more difficult because of general public ignorance and congressional indifference about Africa.

For the American public in general, and even for close students of foreign affairs, Africa was essentially an undiscovered continent until five or six years ago. Since then a degree of awareness has developed, but it is accompanied by great areas of ignorance and consequently by markedly unstable attitudes. Nor have particular groups developed the degree of concern which might have been expected. The American Negro community, while increasingly aware of developments in Africa, remains essentially preoccupied with the civil rights struggle in the United States. American labor and religious groups, which might have been expected to be deeply stirred by the moral and humanitarian aspects of various situations in southern Africa, have been relatively mute and inattentive. American business activities and investment in Africa, though growing, are to a considerable extent centered in South Africa, the heartland of white supremacy.

In both Houses of the American Congress indifference if not ignorance about Africa is painfully evident, apart from a few outstanding individuals such as Representatives O'Hare of Illinois and Bolton of Ohio. Congressmen with a serious, knowledgeable and constructive interest in Africa are extremely few. Even in the Senate Foreign Relations Committee, for example, it has been difficult in recent years to find a member sufficiently concerned about Africa to fill the position of chairman of the Sub-Committee on Africa. The fact that the Sub-Committee has met most infrequently strengthens the general impression that the American Congress, even in a time of great stress in Africa, remains uninterested.

Southern Africa presents a situation in which a stitch in time can save many times nine. It is also one in which realistically the vigor and effectiveness of our actions will depend to a great degree on the courage and perception of the officials of the Department of State. Their reward will be in very large part a shower of criticism from all sides in the United States, at least in the short run, and less than unanimous approval from abroad. In the coming years it can probably be said that the willingness of the Department to take a lonely and unpopular stand on many issues in southern Africa, and to persevere in convincing the President and the Congress, will determine the extent to which the long-term needs and interests of the American republic in that area are served.

The Stakes and Prospects over the Longer Term

In the years immediately ahead, a series of dramatic happenings is likely to force the problems of southern Africa to the forefront of world, and therefore of American, concern. To some extent the pace may be forced by growing Soviet and Chinese intervention. But apart from this, other powerful pressures—particularly racial resentment—will drive events toward climax. It seems probable, therefore, that however reluctant it may be to expand its commitments in Africa, the United States will be drawn more and more deeply into the situation.

The shifting course of events will give rise to wide swings of mood about Africa. The conduct of Africans on occasion will generate tides of exasperation, and outbreaks of civil strife combined with indications of Communist influence will provide effective stimulants to pessimism and fear. For all who like to pontificate on world affairs, Africa will continue to provide a veritable playground: the "realists" will find plentiful pretext for their most extreme proposals for military solutions and the support of reaction; and "idealists" will discover ample basis for their most extravagant proposals for the support of revolution and the massive outlay of humanitarian assistance.

The African revolution has not yet completed even its first phase, and reactions to the disorders to come will be exceptionally erratic because all African events have to be interpreted on the basis of extremely brief experience: practically all the African states are still less than ten years old. The United States will be as susceptible as any country to mercurial shifts of feelings and policy toward Africa; already it has shown a knack for lecturing the Africans about their political adolescence while at the same time indulging in displays of diplomatic immaturity itself.

In such a clamorous and confusing situation it is unusually important to attempt to see the immediate scene in some historical perspective and to identify the policy approaches and longer-term objectives which can give wisdom and continuity to our efforts. First, it is worth remembering that what has happened in recent years in Africa is essentially hopeful. For all the strains and dangers which have resulted from decolonization—a major forward step has been taken in mankind's political evolution.

Second, not as a rigid precept but as a broad guide to conduct, the United States should continue to place its faith in the principle that governments in Africa should rest on the consent, and provide for the participation, of the governed. The advance of independence to date has not increased the appearance of stability in Africa; but there is no convincing reason to think the continent would be less dangerous and disorderly if the attempt had been made to maintain colonial rule. In southern Africa the replacement of white minority governments may be accompanied by further disorders; but there is no reasonable basis to believe that peace or progress would be served by attempts to perpetuate the political subservience of nearly 90 per cent of the population.

Third, all hope of encouraging the evolutionary development of more just and stable political arrangements through nonviolent and moderate means is not lost. As far as U.S. policy is concerned, such methods have hardly been tried. General declarations in behalf of self-determination have been made; but failure to go beyond words and contradictory action in favor of the present white regimes have undercut the credibility of our declarations. The newer instruments of diplomacy have not been fully used in a consistent and coordinated manner.

Moderate measures may of course prove insufficient, especially in view of the lateness of the hour. But they should seriously be tried. The lateness of the hour makes the attempt all the more imperative and urgent. If they fail, then new and grim alternatives may have to be faced. But if they succeed in advancing self-government and racial justice in southern Africa, the consequences will be of immeasurable importance in stabilizing political relations throughout the continent and in assuaging what otherwise could develop into one of the ugliest dangers of the future—race war and the division of the world along the color line. More forthright action in relation to these intermingled moral and political issues would greatly strengthen the prestige and position of the United States throughout all the underdeveloped and non-white areas of the world.

Moreover, such action could do much for the self-respect of the United States itself. For the moral and philosophical aspects of the issues presented by southern Africa touch the deepest chords of national and individual conscience and have powerful implications for our own domestic racial dilemma. By positive contributions to the shaping of change in southern Africa, the United States will advance its objectives and interests around the world. And at the same time it may find invigoration for its own national spirit and strength.

Index

COUNCIL ON FOREIGN RELATIONS

Officers and Directors

John J. McCloy, *Chairman of the Board*
Henry M. Wriston, *Honorary President*
Grayson Kirk, *President*
Frank Altschul, *Vice-President & Secretary*
David Rockefeller, *Vice-President*
Gabriel Hauge, *Treasurer*
George S. Franklin, Jr., *Executive Director*

Hamilton Fish Armstrong
Elliott V. Bell
William P. Bundy
William A. M. Burden
Arthur H. Dean
Allen W. Dulles
Thomas K. Finletter
William C. Foster

Caryl P. Haskins
Joseph E. Johnson
Walter H. Mallory
James A. Perkins
Philip D. Reed
Whitney H. Shepardson
Charles M. Spofford
Carroll L. Wilson

PUBLICATIONS

FOREIGN AFFAIRS (quarterly), edited by Hamilton Fish Armstrong.

THE UNITED STATES IN WORLD AFFAIRS (annual). Volumes for 1931, 1932 and 1933, by Walter Lippmann and William O. Scroggs; for 1934–1935, 1936, 1937, 1938, 1939 and 1940, by Whitney H. Shepardson and William O. Scroggs; for 1945–1947, 1947–1948 and 1948–1949, by John C. Campbell; for 1949, 1950, 1951, 1952, 1953 and 1954, by Richard P. Stebbins; for 1955, by Hollis W. Barber; for 1956, 1957, 1958, 1959, 1960, 1961, 1962 and 1963, by Richard P. Stebbins.

DOCUMENTS ON AMERICAN FOREIGN RELATIONS (annual). Volume for 1952 edited by Clarence W. Baier and Richard P. Stebbins; for 1953 and 1954, edited by Peter V. Curl; for 1955, 1956, 1957, 1958 and 1959, edited by Paul E. Zinner; for 1960, 1961, 1962 and 1963, edited by Richard P. Stebbins.

POLITICAL HANDBOOK AND ATLAS OF THE WORLD (annual), edited by Walter H. Mallory.

REMNANTS OF EMPIRE: The United Nations and the End of Colonialism, by David W. Wainhouse.

THE EUROPEAN COMMUNITY AND AMERICAN TRADE: A Study in Atlantic Economics and Policy, by Randall Hinshaw.

THE FOURTH DIMENSION OF FOREIGN POLICY: Educational and Cultural Affairs, by Philip H. Coombs.

AMERICAN AGENCIES INTERESTED IN INTERNATIONAL AFFAIRS (Fifth Edition), compiled by Donald Wasson.

JAPAN AND THE UNITED STATES IN WORLD TRADE, by Warren S. Hunsberger.

FOREIGN AFFAIRS BIBLIOGRAPHY, 1952–1962, by Henry L. Roberts.

THE DOLLAR IN WORLD AFFAIRS: An Essay in International Financial Policy, by Henry G. Aubrey.

ON DEALING WITH THE COMMUNIST WORLD, by George F. Kennan.

FOREIGN AID AND FOREIGN POLICY, by Edward S. Mason.

THE SCIENTIFIC REVOLUTION AND WORLD POLITICS, by Caryl P. Haskins.

AFRICA: A Foreign Affairs Reader, edited by Philip W. Quigg.

THE PHILIPPINES AND THE UNITED STATES: Problems of Partnership, by George E. Taylor.

SOUTHEAST ASIA IN UNITED STATES POLICY, by Russell H. Fifield.

UNESCO: ASSESSMENT AND PROMISE, by George N. Shuster.

THE PEACEFUL ATOM IN FOREIGN POLICY, by Arnold Kramish.

THE ARABS AND THE WORLD: Nasser's Arab Nationalist Policy, by Charles D. Cremeans.

TOWARD AN ATLANTIC COMMUNITY, by Christian A. Herter.

THE SOVIET UNION, 1922–1962: A Foreign Affairs Reader, edited by Philip E. Mosely.

THE POLITICS OF FOREIGN AID: American Experience in Southeast Asia, by John D. Montgomery.

SPEARHEADS OF DEMOCRACY: Labor in the Developing Countries, by George C. Lodge.

LATIN AMERICA: Diplomacy and Reality, by Adolf A. Berle.

THE ORGANIZATION OF AMERICAN STATES AND THE HEMISPHERE CRISIS, by John C. Dreier.

THE UNITED NATIONS: Structure for Peace, by Ernest A. Gross.

THE LONG POLAR WATCH: Canada and the Defense of North America, by Melvin Conant.

ARMS AND POLITICS IN LATIN AMERICA (Revised Edition), by Edwin Lieuwen.

THE FUTURE OF UNDERDEVELOPED COUNTRIES: Political Implications of Economic Development (Revised Edition), by Eugene Staley.

SPAIN AND DEFENSE OF THE WEST: Ally and Liability, by Arthur P. Whitaker.

SOCIAL CHANGE IN LATIN AMERICA TODAY: Its Implications for United States Policy, by Richard N. Adams, John P. Gillin, Allan R. Holmberg, Oscar Lewis, Richard W. Patch, and Charles W. Wagley.

FOREIGN POLICY: THE NEXT PHASE: The 1960s (Revised Edition), by Thomas K. Finletter.

DEFENSE OF THE MIDDLE EAST: Problems of American Policy (Revised Edition), by John C. Campbell.

COMMUNIST CHINA AND ASIA: Challenge to American Policy, by A. Doak Barnett.

FRANCE, TROUBLED ALLY: De Gaulle's Heritage and Prospects, by Edgar S. Furniss, Jr.

THE SCHUMAN PLAN: A Study in Economic Cooperation, 1950–1959, by William Diebold, Jr.

SOVIET ECONOMIC AID: The New Aid and Trade Policy in Underdeveloped Countries, by Joseph S. Berliner.

RAW MATERIALS: A Study of American Policy, by Percy W. Bidwell.

NATO AND THE FUTURE OF EUROPE, by Ben T. Moore.

AFRICAN ECONOMIC DEVELOPMENT, by William Hance.

INDIA AND AMERICA: A Study of Their Relations, by Phillips Talbot and S. L. Poplai.

JAPAN BETWEEN EAST AND WEST, by Hugh Borton, Jerome B. Cohen, William J. Jorden, Donald Keene, Paul F. Langer and C. Martin Wilbur.

NUCLEAR WEAPONS AND FOREIGN POLICY, by Henry A. Kissinger.

MOSCOW-PEKING AXIS: Strength and Strains, by Howard L. Boorman, Alexander Eckstein, Philip E. Mosely and Benjamin Schwartz.

RUSSIA AND AMERICA: Dangers and Prospects, by Henry L. Roberts.

Pol. Sci.

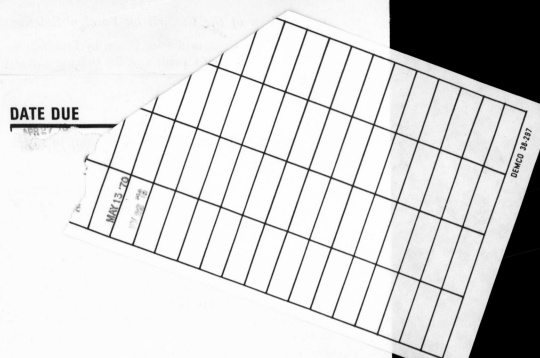